PC/MS-DOS
Made Easy

Tony Dowden

COMPUTE! Publications,Inc.abc

A Capital Cities/ABC, Inc. Company
Greensboro, North Carolina

Dedication

This book is dedicated to my wife—Patty—who tolerated the long hours it took to get this book to press. Next time, we move the computer out of the bedroom.

Printed in the United States of America

10 9 8 7 6 5 4 3 2 1

ISBN 0-87455-138-2

COMPUTE! Publications, Inc., Post Office Box 5406, Greensboro, NC 27403, (919) 275-9809, is a Capital Cities/ABC, Inc. company, and is not associated with any manufacturer of personal computers. IBM PC and PC-DOS are trademarks or registered trademarks of International Business Machines Corporation. MS-DOS is a trademark of Microsoft Corporation.

Contents

Foreword

Users of the powerful personal computers—the IBM PC line and PC compatibles—have been provided with an operating system that is constantly being improved. Its latest version, DOS 3.3, is a marvel of power and efficiency. But to the beginning user, or to the user interested in improving the way the computer system operates, it can be an extremely complicated maze of switches, filters, directories, and blind alleys.

Tony Dowden's book, *PC/MS-DOS Made Easy*, provides information both about DOS in general and about DOS 3.3 in particular. In it, you will discover a full explanation of DOS commands (with particular attention to the commands most frequently used), full instructions on writing batch files to make your use of the computer as efficient and trouble-free as possible, and a list of all error messages and instructions for dealing with them.

There's also a discussion of powerful programs—some of which can be had free of charge, others which can be obtained at a very low cost. A list of distributors of this software is also provided.

Written in friendly, everyday language, *PC/MS-DOS Made Easy* only assumes a general familiarity with the MS-DOS computer. If you are familiar with the PC keyboard, the care and handling of floppy disks, and how to turn on your computer, you're ready for this text. You won't believe how easy it is to provide yourself with your own set of specialized commands through the use of simple batch files. This book even provides a do-it-yourself menu-driven user interface that allows you to access files and run utilities by entering a single keystroke. With *PC/MS-DOS Made Easy*, you'll be able to use your computer like a pro.

Acknowledgments

I first must thank my wife for the hours she spent in reading, commenting, and sweating over this book. Behind every successful writer there must be a spouse or partner so dedicated.

I must also thank the cats of the world, those unsung heroes of the writer's life, who keep the feet of writers warm on long cold nights—so the work keeps flowing.

Chapter 1

Introduction

Chapter 1

Introduction

Welcome to the world of PC-DOS and MS-DOS, especially to version 3.3. Throughout the rest of this book, for easier reading, PC-DOS version 3.3 and MS-DOS version 3.3 will be referred to simply as DOS.

Although *PC/MS-DOS Made Easy* contains a wealth of information that will apply to most versions of DOS, it principally covers version 3.3. Where a DOS 3.3 enhancement is discussed, you'll be told, so if you have an earlier version that doesn't include the command or if the command doesn't work, you'll know why. In addition, some computer manufacturers have contracted with Microsoft to include MS-DOS with their computers. Often, these manufacturers make enhancements that are covered in their own documentation. Though these enhancements rarely conflict with normal MS-DOS operation, you should consult your system documentation in those few cases where information presented here conflicts with the operation of your system.

PC/MS-DOS Made Easy is written for the first-day computer user. It's written for the person who has little or no familiarity with PC-DOS or MS-DOS. It's assumed that you know how to turn on your computer and how to handle floppy disks. It's also assumed that you are familiar with the location of the keys on the keyboard. But you may have never used a computer running the PC-DOS or MS-DOS operating system, or you may be taking an introductory course in computers and want more information on using the DOS environment.

CHAPTER 1

This book is a supplement to your DOS documentation, to help you understand DOS and make it easier to use. Consequently, there are some little-used commands that intentionally are not covered in depth in this book. This book will take you from being a new user, or one who is uncomfortable with DOS, to being a user who is comfortable with DOS and who uses the fundamental commands easily. Power users, who need to know every nuance of every command, should refer to the manuals that came with their copy of DOS.

Of all the operating systems in use today on micro computers, PC-DOS and MS-DOS are the most common. Thanks to the efforts of IBM, Microsoft, and the dozens of clone-makers, the PC-DOS and MS-DOS operating systems are used by millions of people throughout the world. In spite of such widespread distribution, confusion about how to use it often results in use of only a few restricted commands or in misuse that results in loss of data. One of the goals of this book is to help you through this confusion. DOS has many features and great power, but it can also be easy to use. All it takes is a few hours learning DOS, some decent batch files and procedures, and you will have the computer system you want.

This book has many examples, and much information in a problem-solution format. You'll be shown which commands do what, and in the case of batch files, you'll see how to alter the examples provided to suit your needs. Most examples are taken from real life, directly from systems in daily use for many years in various forms, rather than from an ideal system created solely for the purpose of writing a book.

Chapter 2 provides instruction for the beginning user. It will tell you what to look for and what to look out for when you first begin to use your machine. You will read about system commands, booting up, peripherals, and so on. Of course, if you are already a computer user, you may skip this chapter, but if your experience with IBM PCs and compatibles is limited, you may discover some things in this chapter that you didn't know before.

Chapter 3, "How DOS Works," is written for the person with little knowledge of computers, and it covers some basics of the DOS operating system. You can skip this chapter if you wish, but you'll find information there that will help you understand other parts of the book. Besides, it's a short chapter. And you will probably agree that the few minutes it takes to read it are well spent.

Chapter 4, "Hard Disks and Floppies," gives you a brief introduction to the world of disk drives and disks. Since the purpose of this book is to show how easy DOS is to use, topics like sectors, tracks, and formats will be avoided (if you would like to read about these topics in depth, consider purchasing the book *Hard Disk Management*, also from COMPUTE! Books). You'll find enough information in Chapter 4 to help you understand what a disk is and how much it holds, and the technical material will be left to the technical books.

Chapter 5, "Using DOS," provides a brief question-and-answer section covering the most elementary uses of DOS. The details are left for subsequent chapters, but this chapter will get you started.

Chapter 6, "DOS Commands," discusses each of the DOS commands and how the keyboard editing keys can be used.

Chapter 7, "Batch Files," shows you how to use batch files. This chapter presents the basics.

Chapter 8, "The CONFIG.SYS File," covers using this file to make your computer easier to use and more powerful.

Chapter 9, "Using EDLIN," shows you how to use the editor that comes with DOS. Although most people use a more powerful text-editor program for word processing or programming, EDLIN works well for making quick changes to Batch files, CONFIG.SYS files, and short editing work.

CHAPTER 1

Chapter 10, "Using DEBUG," shows you how to use the program DEBUG, a programmer's tool provided with some versions of DOS. Although professional programmers may opt to buy more powerful tools, DEBUG is a very capable program development tool.

Chapter 11, "The AUTOEXEC.BAT File," discusses the AUTOEXEC.BAT file, how to create it, and some of the things you can do to make your computer operation smoother.

Chapter 12, "DOS Techniques," takes you through a number of typical tasks in the operation of a PC and tells you simple ways to perform those tasks more effectively. Most of these procedures involve the use of batch files.

Chapter 13, "A DOS Shell," shows you how to create a menu-driven program using simple batch files that will make your computer easier to use.

Chapter 14 will provide information that can only be used by experienced users. But by the time you have read to Chapter 14, you should be able to understand all of the information in it. Batch files are like programs, and this chapter expands this concept by explaining how to branch and loop within a batch file, as well as provide user input.

Appendix A, "Public Domain and Shareware Software," explains these types of programs and lists some places where you can get them.

Appendix B, "List of Files," provides you with a listing of the files included in the distribution disks of DOS 3.3 from IBM.

Appendix B, "List of Files," provides you with a listing of the files included in the distribution disks of DOS 3.3 from IBM.

Appendix C," DOS Commands," reviews all of the DOS commands in alphabetical order.

Appendix D, "DOS Editing Keys," is a review of the uses of the function and other editing keys. It is a quick reference so you won't have to go searching through text to find out how to perform these functions.

Appendix E, "Error Messages," lists some of the error messages you might encounter, along with the cause of

6

the error and what you can do to eliminate the problem. Since a complete listing of all the error messages would be a book in itself, I have shown only the ones normally encountered.

Conventions

Before you get into the rest of the book, there are a few things you need to know. In talking about DOS, you need to use certain conventions, explained here.

The Enter key. In this book, you will often encounter text that resembles the following:

DIR[Enter]

This means type *DIR* and then press the Enter key on your keyboard.

The Ctrl or Control key. The control key is used, like a shift key, to add more functions to the keys on the keyboard. Pressing the control key changes the functions of the keys and is often used by programs for control functions. Throughout this book

Ctrl-Z

means press the Ctrl key and hold it down while pressing the letter Z. (You don't have to hold the Shift key as well. Uppercase is used here to make the book easier to read.)

The prefix *Ctrl-* simply means press the Ctrl key, just as you would the Shift key, before pressing the indicated letter, and release it after releasing the indicated letter. In the same manner

Ctrl-S

means press the Ctrl key while pressing the letter *S*. The same technique of using the prefix Ctrl- applies to all the other characters on the keyboard.

The * and ? (wildcard) characters. Files are sometimes called using the * and ? characters. The * character is used as a string of wildcards in place of a string of characters, and the ? character is used as a wildcard in place of a single character.

For example, when you want to look through the directory for all of the files with a file type of .COM, you would type

```
DIR *.COM[Enter]
```

This would display all of the files with the file type of .COM.

If you were looking through your directory for all the files with an eight-letter file name ending in ZZ, you might type

```
DIR ??????ZZ.*[Enter]
```

This would list files such as SHOWUPZZ.COM, LISTEDZZ.TXT, or 123456ZZ.CAT. It would not list the files TESTZZ.COM or 12345ZZ.CAT, because in both cases, though the last two letters were ZZ, there were not six characters (letters or numbers) to replace the ? characters in the list you requested.

Filenames. Throughout the rest of this book, you will read about files often, such as when copying and erasing them is discussed. A symbolic reference will be used. When the reference *fn.ft* is used, it means *filename.file type*. Substitute the name and type of the file you are using.

Disk drives. There are many possible configurations of computers running DOS. Some may have only one floppy disk drive, some two, some may have a hard disk and one or two floppy disk drives, and there are a number of different kinds of floppy drives. As a result, this book cannot cover every possible configuration. Throughout the book it is assumed that you have a system with one hard drive, assigned as drive C:, and one or two floppy disk drives, respectively assigned A: and B:. Most of the information in this book also applies to other configurations. Where it won't work with another configuration, you'll be shown a way around the problem.

Variables. Where a number may appear in an example, and the number may vary, it will be represented by the variable <x>. Where the disk drive referred to may be any drive, the variable <x:> will be inserted.

Terms

What follows is a discussion of terms used in the DOS world. This is probably the most difficult part of the book. Once you understand these terms, the rest will be easy. You'll notice that there are only a few terms to learn. That's because there is no reason for you to learn a large amount of computer jargon, and in this book jargon will be kept to a minimum.

BIOS. BIOS stands for Basic Input/Output System. This is a part of the computer system that interfaces the computer hardware to the operating system. The BIOS is a program stored inside the computer, in ROM (Read Only Memory). It acts as an interface between the computer hardware and DOS. The part of the BIOS that talks to the computer is tailored specifically to that particular computer, which is why it is included with the computer. The part that talks to DOS is an industry standard, and is written to adhere to standards defined by Microsoft and IBM.

DOS. DOS stands for Disk Operating System. The prefixes, PC and MS, stand for Personal Computer or Microsoft, respectively. This operating system was initially developed by Microsoft in a joint effort with IBM in response to a need for an operating system that was to be both easy to use and powerful.

Interface. This is a function performed by either hardware or software that allows two dissimilar items to communicate. As an analogy, a steering wheel can be thought of as the interface between the driver and the car. In the context of this book, an interface refers to a piece of software, usually either the BIOS or DOS, that acts as the software interface between you and the computer hardware.

Operating System. The operating system is a software package that interfaces, or connects, the various parts of the computer hardware or BIOS with the software or application programs. This item is present, in one form or another, on virtually every computer system today. Also see Chapter 3, "How DOS Works."

Chapter 2

Your Computer

Chapter 2

Your Computer

Before we can discuss what DOS is all about, and how to use it, you must first understand a little bit about your hardware—what it does and how it interacts with your software.

What Is Hardware?

Hardware includes all the physical components of your computer. This includes the keyboard, the CPU (Central Processing Unit), and the monitor or screen. A few computers incorporate some or all of these components into a single unit. This is typical of a portable unit or a laptop machine.

The makeup of a typical system usually consists of three parts: a keyboard, a CPU and a monitor. These are shown in Figure 2-1.

Figure 2-1. The Contents of a Typical System

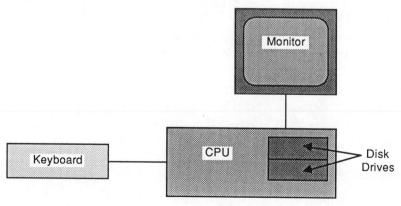

Of the components shown in Figure 2-1, the keyboard and monitor are fairly standard. They consist of a keyboard that sends data, as it is typed, to the CPU. (If you are technically oriented, you might be interested to know the data is serial ASCII, 8 bits, no parity, and one stop bit.)

The monitor. The monitor is usually either monochrome (single color, usually green or amber) or color. Color monitors come in two general categories: RGB style, such as is found on CGA-equipped systems, and TTL or analog monitors, as are found on EGA-, PGA-, or VGA-equipped systems. It seems as if someone offers a new video standard about every week, so it wouldn't be productive to discuss them in any detail. CGA systems usually display 640 × 200 pixels, or dots, per screen. This results in color of high enough quality for playing games, and fair enough quality for text. The EGA and better systems display 640 × 350 or 640 × 480 pixels, and, along with better graphics, the text is much improved. In addition, several companies have added new modes to the computer with some very high-resolution monochrome displays, and desktop publishing has pushed the needs, and availabilities, to over 1024 × 1024 pixels. This allows the computer to display as many as 170 columns by 113 rows of text.

The CPU. The CPU gets even more complex. There, you have a choice of these processors: 8088, 8086, 80186, 80286, 80386, and some compatible variations. There are also coprocessors, components that take over the math functions and perform them much more efficiently than the processor can. Here there are the 8087, the 80287, and the 80387, and a number of very powerful and specialized coprocessors. And then there is also processor memory. You have a choice of the amount of memory, from 256K (that's about 256,000 bytes, or characters) up to 4 gigabytes, which is the memory the new 80386 processor can address directly.

Mass storage. There's also mass storage, usually in the form of floppy and hard disks. Floppy disks normally store either 360K or 1.2 megabytes (1200K). Hard disks are awesomely large, starting at 10 megabytes and going up to over 300 megabytes. Even larger hard disk drives are on the horizon, and you can have more than one hard disk or floppy disk drive in your system. Most computers only have room for two floppy disk drives and a hard disk, though some can handle as many as six drives in any combination.

Plus, there are hundreds of printers, covering the range from dot-matrix to formed-character to laser printers. And there are a number of modems. A modem is a device that allows you to connect your computer system to the phone lines and access other computer systems throughout the world. For accessing other computers that are close, usually within the same building, there are LANs (Local Area Networks) that not only allow you access to the information on another computer's disk drive, but even allow you to run software on the other computer system.

What Is Software?

Software is the code, the programs, you load into your computer to make the computer do something. Inside your computer is a type of memory called *ROM*. Inside ROM is some very important software called the *BIOS* that ties together the computer's hardware and the software. Just how this happens is beyond the scope of this book, but in general terms it defines a set of standards which, if met by both the hardware and software companies, assures that the hardware and software will be able to talk to each other. It also assures that software that runs on one machine will run on all machines. Unfortunately this isn't always the case.

The next step in software, beyond the BIOS, is the operating system. For the purpose of this book, the operating system is DOS. There are other operating systems available for personal computers, most notably the UNIX operating system, but none has proved as popular in the world of IBM PCs and compatibles as MS-DOS.

Beyond the operating system are the applications programs. These consist of everything from games to word processors to spreadsheets to databases to desktop publishing to drawing and engineering aids and so on almost indefinitely. There is virtually no limit to what is available because the computer's capabilities are only limited by the imaginations of the programmers. If what you want isn't available, there are dozens of programming languages and armies of programmers who can create just what you want—for a fee, of course.

That's what computers are all about. They do work for you, and they do it more quickly and more accurately than almost any human can.

Turning on the System

Turning on the system is quite easy. You just flip the power switch, usually on the side of the computer, up or to the ON position. In addition, you will need to make sure that the monitor, and any peripherals you use, are also turned on.

The computer first goes into a self-test mode. This is usually invisible to you, since the computer rarely displays a message unless it finds something wrong. This self-test includes a test of the keyboard, a test of the internal memory, and tests to determine what types of accessories you have installed. If errors are found, the computer usually provides some kind of indication. The system response will vary depending on which machine you have. Some computers lock up and refuse to go any further, some display messages telling what the problem is, and some automatically run programs that either fix the problem or determine what the problem is in order to fix it later. Every computer is different, and you will have to consult your user manual to determine what your system is designed to do.

Your Computer

After the self-test is completed, the computer goes to a routine where it loads the operating system, DOS. From the information it gained during the self-test phase, it knows what type of hardware is connected to it. The computer first tries to find DOS on floppy disk drive A:. If there is no disk in drive A:, it will try to find DOS on the hard disk (if it found one). Once it has found DOS, it loads it into memory, along with other programs you may have specified. These additional programs are loaded through the use of files called CONFIG.SYS and AUTOEXEC.BAT. Usually, the programs you are adding either are extensions or additions to DOS or are programs that are run after DOS is loaded, providing some added functionality such as calculators or spelling checkers that you can call into action by typing a certain set of keystrokes. Many of these programs can be called even while you are running other programs.

Later in this book you will be shown in detail how to alter your AUTOEXEC.BAT and CONFIG.SYS files to load new programs.

Taking Care of Your System

There are several things to watch when taking care of your system. The first enemy of computer hardware is dust. If the fan on the back of your CPU has a filter, clean it regularly. How often you clean it depends on how much dust you have in the air, but checking it weekly until you have established a pattern is a good idea.

The keyboard attracts all kinds of contaminants. They include everything from spilled coffee and soda to cookie crumbs and dust. A dust cover over your keyboard can help to extend its life. Cleaning the keyboard periodically will also extend its life. If you don't feel qualified to remove the screws on the back and open it up for a good brushing (and it's perfectly legitimate to be concerned about damaging the machine while cleaning it), get a technical person to do it for you occasionally.

CHAPTER 2

The second part of maintaining your system is backing up the programs and information on your disks. *Backing up* means copying the information from one disk onto another and storing the copy in a safe place. Later in this book, you'll see several means for doing this. A general rule of thumb is to back up a disk whenever you have done enough work that, if it were lost, you'd be inconvenienced. All disks, either hard or floppy, are susceptible to damage. Hard disks are easily damaged by physical abuse (a surprisingly mild vibration or shock could cause the disk to become gouged, resulting in severe damage, especially if it happens while the system is running). Touching the floppy disk on the shiny part through the oblong window or setting it near an electric motor or in a warm place can cause permanent loss of the data on the disk.

On the other hand, if you place your computer in a cool, dry place that is isolated from vibration and shock, exercise minimal caution with your disks, and are sure to back up your information regularly, you can expect years of virtually trouble-free service from your computer.

Chapter 3
How DOS Works

Chapter 3

How DOS Works

This chapter discusses what DOS is, what it does for you, and how it does it. Referring to Figure 3-1, you can see that DOS is shown as an interface between you and the hardware (disk drives, display, and so on) of the computer. It's also an interface between the software you run, such as a spreadsheet or a word processor, and the hardware of the computer. Let's look at just what the DOS interface does.

In order to show what DOS is, start by thinking about a typical operation: displaying the files that are on the computer's disk drives. To display a list of the files, type the command

DIR[Enter]

The command, DIR, tells the hardware, specifically the disk drive (through the BIOS), to read its directory. Once the disk drive has told DOS what it contains, DOS sends the information to the display hardware, which displays the information on the screen.

When you run an application program, such as a spreadsheet or a word processor, the software loads from the disk drive into the computer's memory. For example, if you want to load BASIC, type

BASIC[Enter]

DOS takes these commands from the keyboard (through the BIOS) and tells the disk drive (through the BIOS) to load BASIC into the computer's memory. Next, BASIC sends a message through DOS to the display circuitry and the screen telling you that BASIC is ready to use. You

Figure 3-1. The Computer's Software Structure

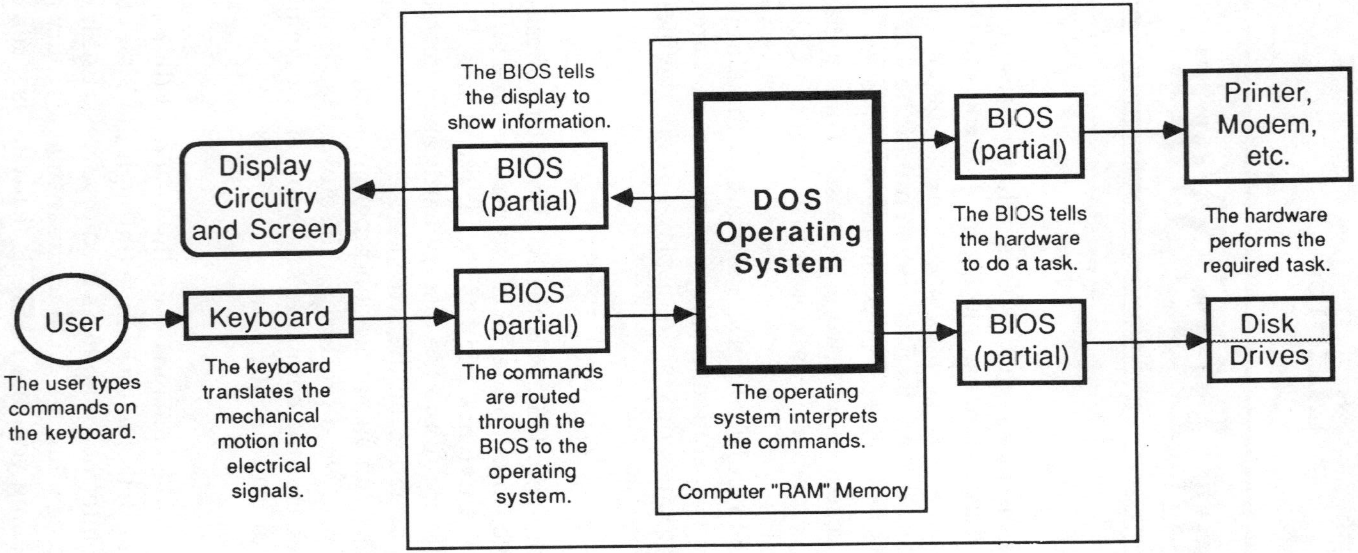

Printer, Modem, etc.

Disk Drives

The hardware performs the required task.

BIOS (partial)

The BIOS tells the hardware to do a task.

BIOS (partial)

DOS Operating System

The operating system interprets the commands.

Computer "RAM" Memory

The BIOS tells the display to show information.

BIOS (partial)

BIOS (partial)

The commands are routed through the BIOS to the operating system.

Display Circuitry and Screen

Keyboard

The keyboard translates the mechanical motion into electrical signals.

User

The user types commands on the keyboard.

then respond by typing a command on the keyboard, telling BASIC what to do, and DOS sends the command to BASIC.

If this seems like a lot of manipulating and maneuvering, it is. But there is a very good reason for it. All computer manufacturers build their hardware products with different components and characteristics. If it weren't for this arrangement, it would be necessary for software developers to make a different version for each type of computer—a horrendous task.

The solution is to divide the interface functions between a software side (DOS) and a hardware side (BIOS). BIOS provides custom communications for the different machines each manufacturer builds. DOS provides a standard software interface for the applications programs to talk to without concerning themselves with the question of how the hardware will actually accomplish a given task.

Drives. Disk drives are usually assigned letters. Most systems adhere to these conventions. The following shows typical drive configurations and their letter assignments:

Letter	Drive
A	First floppy disk drive
B	Second floppy disk drive
C	First hard disk drive
D	Second hard disk or ramdisk

If you have a system with a hard disk, the normal procedure is to have DOS on it. When you turn the machine on, BIOS looks for DOS on the A: drive, and if one is there, it will load DOS into memory from that disk. If there is no disk in the A: drive, BIOS will look for a C: drive. If there is a C: drive, BIOS assumes it is a hard disk, and it will load DOS from there. In this manner, you can always load DOS from a floppy disk if your hard disk has a problem.

If BIOS fails to find DOS on any of the drives, BIOS will display an error message on the screen, and you'll have to insert a system disk into one of the floppy drives and then press a key or reset the computer (the screen will tell you what to do).

If your system doesn't have a hard disk, BIOS first looks for an A: drive from which to load DOS; if it fails to find it, it looks for a B: drive. As above, if BIOS fails to find DOS on either the A: or B: drives, it will display an error message. In that case, you'll need to insert a disk into one of the drives, then either press a key or reset the computer.

Once you are logged onto a drive, the computer will display a prompt. This is an indication that the computer is ready to be used. Typical prompts look like:

A:

or

C:

The appearance of the prompt can be changed, and in fact can be used to display useful information. This will be covered in the discussion of the PROMPT command in Chapter 11.

To change to another drive (this is often called *logging onto another drive*), simply type the drive letter followed by a colon and the Enter key. For example, if you are on the C: drive and want to change to the A: drive, you type:

A:[Enter]

The prompt, assuming you have a standard prompt, will change from C: to A:.

Sometimes you may have programs on one drive that you need to use with other programs or data on another drive. If, for example, you are logged onto drive C: and you want to run a program (in the following example, called TEST) on the A: drive, you would type the following:

A:TEST[Enter]

This tells DOS to go to drive A: and run the program called TEST. After the program runs, you would (normally) be returned to drive C:.

Another example is looking at the directory of another drive. Instead of logging onto that drive, you can tell DOS to look at the desired directory on the other drive. In the following example, I assume you are logged onto drive C: and want to look at the directory of drive A:. Type

DIR A:[Enter]

DOS knows to perform the DIR (directory) command, looking for the directory of drive A:. You will remain logged onto drive C:.

Later on in this book, you will find more examples of using multiple drives, including some shortcuts.

Directories. Directories are areas on the computer's disks where you store information about which files are on the disk and where they are located.

Figure 3-2 shows a typical directory structure. DOS starts at the top in a directory called the ROOT directory. From there, you use DOS commands to move through the directories to the files and programs you need. The organization shown in Figure 3-2 is just an example.

Let's look at some of the directories.

ROOT directory. This is the main directory where the computer starts each time it is turned on. It may call up programs (utilities) from other directories, but it usually returns here, waiting to be told what to do next.

WORDPROC directory. This directory contains three subdirectories. The first contains the *WordStar* word processing program. The second contains all the files for work currently in progress. That might include a book, letters to the publisher, and letters in progress to friends. The third is an archive subdirectory that contains files of completed work, but work that may come in handy from time to time. It may include old contracts, past letters to friends, and magazine articles or fiction pieces that have

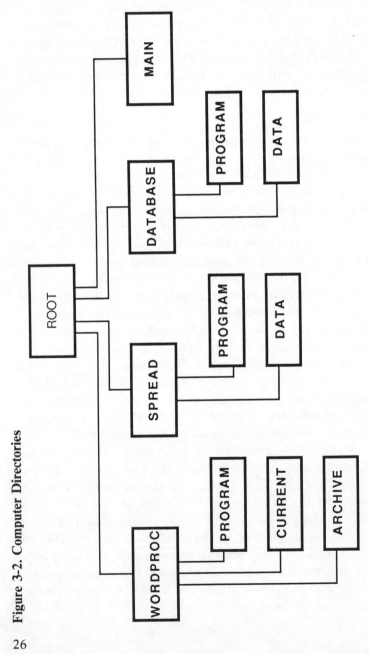

Figure 3-2. Computer Directories

been set aside. Subdirectories work just like directories and may contain subdirectories of their own.

SPREAD directory. This directory contains two subdirectories. The first contains a spreadsheet program, and the second contains spreadsheet files and templates used to keep track of accounts receivable and payable, tax records, and other miscellaneous applications.

DATABASE directory. This directory also contains two subdirectories. The first contains a database program, and the second contains the data files that hold the names, addresses, and phone numbers of friends and business associates, a record library index, and a book collection card file.

MAIN directory. This directory contains programs run occasionally for utility or entertainment. It includes games, communications programs, and general-purpose utilities.

It would be possible to put all of the programs and files in the same directory. However, when the directory is listed, it would be quite large and confusing. By putting each group of programs in a separate directory, it's easy to see what's in each directory. This makes the directory listing less confusing and makes searching for an individual file a logical process. A letter would not be in the DATABASE directory. A game wouldn't be in the WORDPROC directory.

Directories will be discussed again later, along with the PATH command and some of the batch commands.

Filenames and Types. DOS has firm standards for names of files. A filename consists of a name from 1 to 8 characters long, a period, and a file type identifier, or extension, (the period and extension are optional) from 0 to

3 characters long. The filename can consist of any combination of numbers and letters. You can also use some punctuation characters in a filename, but some, such as

```
*
?
\
```

represent wildcards and directory paths and must never be used. The following shows the characters not allowed in filenames:

```
.           |
"           <
/           >
\           +
[           =
]           ;
:           ,
```

Any other characters available on your keyboard (without using the Ctrl or Alt keys) are valid and can be used.

The file type can also consist of any combination of numbers and letters, but certain standards have been established for these. Some of these are:

Extension	File Type
.COM	Program file
.EXE	Program file
.BAT	Batch program
.BAS	BASIC program
.TXT	Text files
.DOC	Documentation files
.OVR	Overlay files used with program files
.DAT	Data files

Files ending with a file type of COM, EXE, or BAT are programs that can be run by typing the filename and pressing Enter. The remaining files are used with program files.

Chapter 4

Hard Disks and Floppies

Chapter 4

Hard Disks and Floppies

In the "old days," computers running DOS were simple. They had floppy disks, occasionally accompanied by cassette tape storage, and, more rarely, by a hard disk. All floppy disks were 5¼-inch, and they had a simple format containing about 80,000, or 80K, bytes (the equivalent of about 40 printed pages) of data. Then technology came along and increased the capacity of the disk, first to 180K bytes, then to 360K bytes and then to a whopping 1,200K (1.2 megabytes or 1.2MB), approximately the equivalent of 600 printed pages. At about the same time, the 3½-inch floppy disk came into use, first storing about 720K bytes, and then doubling to 1.4MB.

Hard disks were developing at the same time, starting with 10MB versions, approximately the equivalent of 5,000 printed pages. Later they developed into 20MB versions, and then to 40MB, and now there are even versions that store over 300MB.

DOS will allow you to use hard disks of almost any size, but there are some limitations. The main limitation is that DOS normally will only address a hard disk of 32MB. Larger hard disks are partitioned, or divided, to fool the operating system into thinking they are several disks of smaller size. There are also several software programs that allow you to have larger disks if necessary.

Your particular system configuration will affect how some of the information in this book applies to you. For example, some of the information covering the use of extensive directories will not apply if you don't have a hard disk. Let's look at some of the characteristics and differences between the different types of disks.

Floppy Disks

Floppy disks come in two physical types, the common 5¼-inch disk and the newer 3½-inch version. The larger 5¼-inch type normally comes in two storage capacities, either 360K bytes or 1.2MB. The 360K type is normally found on XT-type computers, and the 1.2MB version is found on AT-class machines. The smaller 3½-inch type normally comes with either a 720K or 1.4MB capacity. New technologies, not yet available as of the writing of this book, promise to take the storage capacity of the small 3½-inch type to over 10MB.

The advantages of floppy disks are their low cost and the ease with which they can be used to transport files between machines. Floppy disks are still the method of choice for backing up hard disks (copying the files from the hard disk to the floppy) so that, in the event a hard drive (or another floppy) fails, you have a copy of your work and programs.

Figure 4-1. The Two Types of Floppy Disks

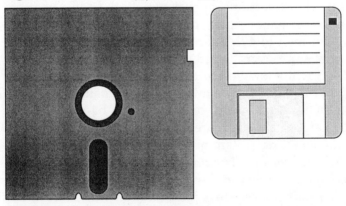

The 5¼-inch *(left)* and 3½-inch floppy disks.

Hard Disks and Floppies

Hard Disks

Hard disks have much higher storage capacity, but they have the disadvantages of being neither interchangeable nor very rugged. Although they boast the ability to withstand an impact, they may not survive a drop of more than a few inches onto a table top. Hard drives in portables are shock-mounted to prevent damage, but even they can be damaged easily.

The best way to ensure that you do not suffer from a hard disk failure is to back up your hard disk. This means copying all the files onto floppy disks as often as it is reasonable to do so. There can be no hard rule to making backups. The best rule of thumb is to back up the files you have changed when the number of changes represent an amount of work you cannot financially or psychologically afford to lose.

Chapter 5

Using DOS

Chapter 5

Using DOS

This brief chapter is for those who don't like to read manuals and prefer to learn by doing. It will take you through a few simple processes just to get you going. The next chapter then details each of the commands in DOS.

What's on the Disk?

Every disk has a directory listing the files stored on the disk. This directory can be read by using a simple command in DOS, DIR, which allows you to see the directory. Type

DIR[Enter]

and DOS will show you what files are stored in the root directory on the disk. Of course, you will not be able to see the files in subdirectories. To look into a subdirectory named FILE, type

DIR \ FILE[Enter]

If you want to see what is on another disk drive, type the drive letter and a colon after the DIR command. For example, to see what is on the disk in drive B:, type

DIR B:[Enter]

DOS will display a listing of all the files on the root directory of the disk in drive B:.

CHAPTER 5

How Much Room Is Left?

The DIR command discussed above will also tell you, after it lists the files, how much room you have on the disk. If you want more information, like what the total storage capacity of the disk is, or how much memory you have free for your programs, type

CHKDSK[Enter]

The CHKDSK program will then tell you how much of the disk you have used and how much is left, as well as how much space you have in the computer's memory for your programs.

Date and Time

Most computers running DOS have date and time capabilities built into the system. When you turn the computer on, it will either automatically read the date and time from an internal clock, or it will ask you for the date and time. This date and time information is available to you at any time by simply typing either

DATE[Enter][Enter]

or

TIME[Enter][Enter]

Note that you press the Enter key twice. When you press it only once, the computer asks you to input the new date or time. The computer will attempt to interpret any keys you press (except Enter) as the new date or time. Often this will result in an error message. If you press Enter twice, you will skip over this prompt. So remember to press Enter twice, unless you mean to change the date or time in the computer.

Copying Files

Files can be copied from one disk to another using the COPY command. This is done by typing COPY followed by the source (from) and destination (to). For example, to copy the file CAT.COM from the disk in the A: drive to the disk in the B: drive, you would type

COPY A:CAT.COM B:CAT.COM[Enter]

Getting Rid of Files

Sometimes you will accumulate too many files on a disk, or your disk will become cluttered with old revisions of a file. To remove some of the files, use either the ERASE or DEL command. DOS uses both interchangeably; they are functionally identical, and you can use whichever is easier for you to remember. To erase a file named CATALOG.TXT, type

ERASE CATALOG.TXT[Enter]

or

DEL CATALOG.TXT[Enter]

The file CATALOG.TXT will be eliminated from the directory, and the space used by the file will be free to be used by other files.

What's in a File?

There will be times when you will need to know what's in a file, but it's too much trouble to load a word processor just to look at the file. Use the TYPE command. The TYPE command allows you to look at the contents of a file, usually a text file, by simply telling DOS to type it on the screen. If you want to look at the contents of a file called CATALOG.TXT, type

TYPE CATALOG.TXT[Enter]

and DOS will display the contents of the file on the screen. Note that this will display the contents of many word processor and editor files, but not all. Some of them use special characters to format of the document, and they will not print correctly on the screen using the TYPE command. In addition, you can also use the TYPE command to look at the contents of any type of file, including a program, though this is of little value. DEBUG does a much better job.

Chapter 6

DOS Commands

Chapter 6

DOS Commands

DOS commands are instructions you give to your computer. These commands might tell the computer to do something with the programs on the disks (load them, run them, alter them, and so on), to alter the computer's characteristics (such as changing to the 40-column text screen), or to perform a task (such as showing the time or a disk directory). Please note that not all the commands listed are available on all versions of DOS. Please refer to your user's manual if you question whether any given command exists on your version.

Types of Commands

There are two types of commands:

• Intrinsic (or resident) commands
• Transient (or disk-resident) commands

Intrinsic commands. Intrinsic commands will work as long as you are at the DOS command-line level (when the DOS prompt is showing). These commands show the contents of a disk's directory, copy and erase files, and so on.

This is a list of intrinsic commands:

BREAK	DEL	RMDIR
CHCP	DIR	SET
CHDIR	ERASE	TIME
CLS	MKDIR	TYPE
COPY	PATH	VER
CTTY	PROMPT	VERIFY
DATE	RENAME	VOL

Transient commands. Transient commands are programs that reside on the disk. They must be loaded from disk before they're executed. The following is a list of the transient commands:

APPEND	JOIN
ASSIGN	KEYB
ATTRIB	LABEL
BACKUP	MODE
BASIC and BASICA	MORE
CHKDSK	NLSFUNC
COMP	PRINT
DEBUG	PROMPT
DISKCOMP	RECOVER
DISKCOPY	REPLACE
EDLIN	RESTORE
EXE2BIN	SELECT
FASTOPEN	SHARE
FDISK	SORT
FIND	SUBST
FORMAT	SYS
GRAFTABL	TREE
GRAPHICS	XCOPY

DOS Commands

The discussion of DOS commands is divided into three parts; those which you will use frequently (virtually every time you run your computer), those which you will use occasionally, and those which you will use seldom, if ever. Of course, your use may be different, but if you use this chapter as a guide as to which commands to learn now and which to learn later, DOS will be easier to learn. Naturally, the more you learn about the commands, and the more often you use them, the easier they will be to use. For many of the commands, you will find examples of their use. Other commands are beyond the scope of this book so will only be mentioned in passing. If you are interested in these relatively complex and technical comands, please refer to your DOS manual for further information.

DOS Commands

Frequently Used Commands

CHDIR or CD	MKDIR or MD
COPY	MORE
DATE	RMDIR or RD,
DEL or ERASE	TIME
DIR	TYPE

Occasionally Used Commands

BACKUP and RESTORE	MODE
CHKDSK	PATH
CLS	RECOVER
FORMAT	REN or RENAME

Seldom Used Commands

APPEND	KEYB
ASSIGN	LABEL
ATTRIB	NLSFUNC
BREAK	PROMPT
CHCP	REPLACE
COMMAND	SELECT
COMP	SET
CTTY	SHARE
DISKCOMP	SORT
DISKCOPY	SUBST
EXE2BIN	SYS
FASTOPEN	TREE
FDISK	VER
FIND	VERIFY
GRAFTABL	VOL
GRAPHICS	XCOPY
JOIN	

CHAPTER 6

DOS Editing Keys

Before getting into a detailed discussion of the DOS commands, here is a way to use some of the editing keys to make the DOS commands easier to use. The location of the keys discussed below are shown in Figure 6-1 (they're shaded in gray). The drawing shows a typical keyboard; yours may differ since there are so many different manufacturers. However, the keys shaded in gray are on your keyboard somewhere.

The DOS editing keys are simply a group of keys that allow you to use DOS faster. They don't edit files, nor do they act as a word processor.

When you are in DOS (and are not running an application), the screen will display a prompt (something like A> or C>). DOS is waiting for you to tell it to do something. You do so by typing a command line.

Anything you type is stored in an area of the computer's memory called a *buffer*. If you type DIR C: to see what's in the directory of drive C:, these characters go into the buffer. Think of the buffer as a storage area, where DOS remembers the last command you typed into the computer. The DOS editing keys can be used to manipulate the information in the buffer.

For example, you can reenter the same line you typed before by pressing the F3 key. If you just looked at the directory, but forgot to look for a file and wanted to display the directory again, then instead of typing the command line

DIR C:[Enter]

you can simply type press the F3 key and then Enter. The F3 key causes the computer to take the characters in the buffer and enter them into the command line. The following paragraphs discuss each of the editing keys in more detail.

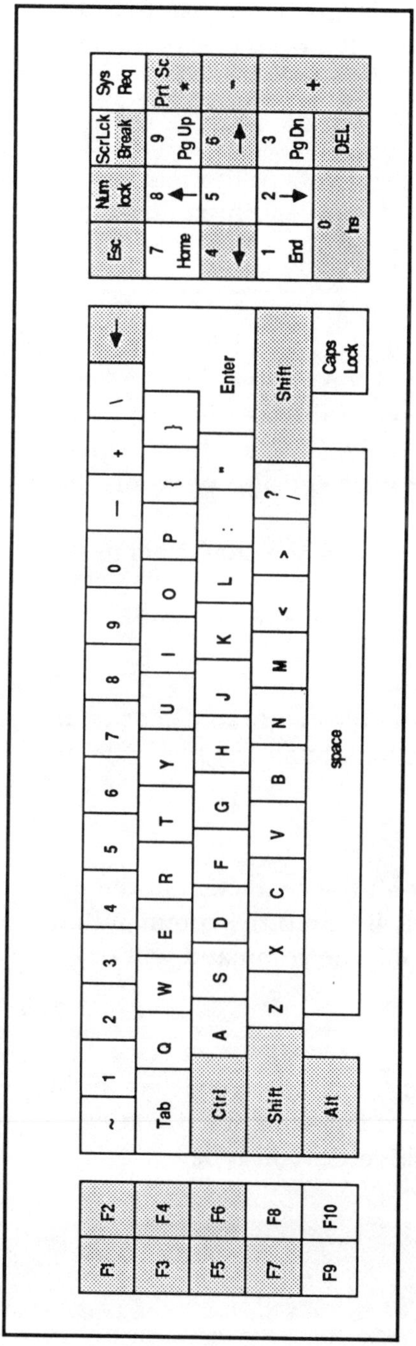

Figure 6-1. DOS Editing Keys

CHAPTER 6

The F1 key. This key repeats one keystroke from the previously typed command line. For example, if you are at the A: prompt and type

DIR C:[Enter]

the computer will display the contents of the root directory on drive C:. If you press the F1 key three times, the screen displays

DIR

You then can type a space and A: and then press Enter to see the directory of the A: disk drive. The F1 key simply repeats the keys you typed the last time you typed an entry on the command line, beginning with the first key in the buffer. The right cursor key also performs this function.

The F2 key. This key copies all the characters in the buffer onto the command line until it reaches a specified key. For example, if you typed the command line

DIR B:*.COM

the first time, to look at all the files with an extension of .COM, and now you want to look at all the files with an extension of .EXE, type

[F2]**.EXE[Enter]

The computer will copy all the characters in the buffer up to the asterisk (DIR B:*) into the command line. You then type *.EXE[Enter] and the command will be sent to the computer as

DIR B:*.EXE

The F3 key. This key copies all the characters in the buffer onto the command line. For example, if you want to look at the directory on drive C:, you type

DIR C:[Enter]

The computer will then display the directory of drive C:. If you forgot to look for a file and wanted to display the directory again, instead of typing the command DIR C: and pressing Enter again, you can simply type

[F3][Enter]

The F3 key enters all the characters in the buffer into the command line.

The F4 key. This key deletes all the characters in the buffer until it reaches a specified key. For example, if you typed the command line

DIR B:TEST.*

to look at all the files with a filename of TEST.*, and now you want to erase all of them, type

DEL [F4]B[F3][Enter]

After you've typed DEL, pressing F4 and typing *B* deletes all characters in the buffer up to the *B*. Pressing F3 enters all the remaining characters into the command line.

The F5 key. This key copies the contents of the command line as it appears on the screen to the buffer. The old contents of the buffer are lost.

The Del key. Pressing this key deletes characters in the command line at the location of the cursor. The left cursor key also performs this function.

The Esc key. This key cancels the current command line. For example, if you get to the end of the command line and realize that you are doing the wrong thing (looking at the directory when you should be changing directories, for instance), pressing the Esc key will take you back to the starting point.

The Ins key. Pressing this key turns on insert mode. Normally when you type a character, the character "types over" the characters already in the buffer. Insert mode allows you to insert characters into the buffer without destroying the characters already in it.

CHAPTER 6

Additional Keys

In addition to the previous keys, there are a number of additional key combinations that perform certain functions in DOS. These are mostly keys that are used in combination, holding down the Shift key or the Ctrl key while pressing one of the other keys. These key combinations are:

The Ctrl-Alt-+ key combination. Pressing the Ctrl, Alt, and + keys at the same time turns up the volume of the keyboard click. Hold the keys down until the keyboard click is at the volume level you want.

The Ctrl-Alt-− key combination. Pressing the Ctrl, Alt, and − (minus) keys at the same time turns down the volume of the keyboard click.

The F6 key. Pressing this key has the same action as Ctrl-Z: It enters a character known as the end of file marker. If you were entering a list of commands from the keyboard to be used by the computer as a batch file, the F6 or Ctrl-Z would be the last character entered. Batch files will be discussed in full later in this book.

The F7 key. Pressing this key results in the same action as Ctrl-@. This causes a NUL character to be entered into the command line.

The Ctrl-Break key combination. This key combination cancels operation of a program in progress. Since the program in progress could be writing to a disk drive, which, if instantly abandoned, could result in destruction of data, this combination should be considered an emergency procedure only.

The Ctrl–Num Lock key combination. This key combination temporarily halts operation of a program in progress. This is handy for stopping information, such as a directory listing, that is scrolling off the screen too fast. Pressing any key causes the operation of the program you were running to resume where it left off.

The Shift-PrtSc key combination. This key combination prints the contents of the screen on the printer. When this is happening, the remaining operations, such as the execution of any programs, are halted. Note that this usually only works with text information, not graphics. If you need to print graphics information, consult your DOS manuals to see if you have special provisions for this, or check with your computer dealer. In addition, there are public domain software sources listed in the back of this book which may have software that will allow you to do this.

The Ctrl-PrtSc key combination. This key combination prints the characters displayed on the screen to the printer at the same time as they are displayed on the screen. This does not dump the entire screen to the printer, only the characters that are displayed after the Ctrl-PrtSc keys are pressed.

The Tab key. This key moves the cursor to the next tab position. The tabs in DOS are normally set at every eighth column.

Frequently Used Commands

The following sections list the commands you are likely to use many times a day. These commands let you move around through the directories, change the date and time, delete files, look at what's in the directory, create and delete directories, and list the contents of some types of files.

The CHDIR or CD command. This command is used to change from one directory to another. You can use either CD or CHDIR—the commands are identical. CD is easier (faster) to type, though CHDIR (CHange DIRectory) is easier to remember for some people. Figure 6-2 shows you how to move from one directory to another.

Note that in Figure 6-2 the use of the slash and the double periods varies depending on whether you are in the root directory or one of the subdirectories. Suppose you are in the root directory, where the computer normally starts, and you want to move to the directory called MAIN, where you have stored your utility programs. Since the MAIN directory is one level below the root directory, all you need to do is type

CD MAIN[Enter]

Figure 6-2. Moving Between Directories

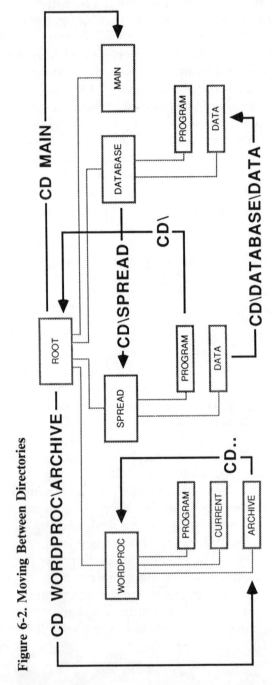

You will then be in the root directory.

But what if you wanted to go from the root directory to the ARCHIVE directory, a subdirectory of the WORDPROC directory? This is the directory where files are stored that you need occasionally, but that you don't want in the way when you are working. To get to the ARCHIVE subdirectory, type

`CD WORDPROC\ARCHIVE[Enter]`

This tells the computer to change directories, through the WORDPROC directory, to the ARCHIVE directory. Once you're there, list the directory. You'll discover that the file you wanted isn't there. So, you have to move back up to the WORDPROC directory and see if it is there. To do that, type

`CD ..[Enter]`

The computer will take you back up one level through the directories. That's what the two periods mean. If, instead of going from the subdirectory to the directory directly above it, you want to go to the root directory, you can type

`CD \[Enter]`

This tells the computer to change directories, and the \ tells the computer to go directly to the root directory.

The COPY command. This command is used every time you copy files from one disk to another or make copies of files in different directories. You may need to load new programs onto your hard disk, to make copies of disks to store in a safe place, or a copy of a new program you wrote for a friend.

The syntax of the COPY command is:

`COPY source destination[Enter]`

The word *source* stands for the file you are copying and the word *destination* stands for the new file you are creating.

CHAPTER 6

You don't always need to specify the destination file. When you don't, the destination file will have the same name as the source file. Since you cannot have two files in the same directory with the same name, you would have to specify the directory or drive where the destination file should appear. For example, if you need to copy files from your floppy disk (drive A:) to your hard disk (drive C:), you would type

COPY A:*.* C:[Enter]

This would copy all of the files in the root directory of drive A: to drive C:. If you want to copy only the .COM files, type

COPY A:*.COM C:[Enter]

If you want to copy the files into a specific directory on the C: drive, you can do it two ways. One (if you are not logged onto drive C:) is to log onto the C: drive by typing

C:[Enter]

Then you log into the directory you want to transfer the files to (in this example, MAIN) by typing

CD MAIN[Enter]

Once you're logged into the MAIN directory on the C: drive, type the command

COPY A:*.*[Enter]

and all the files in the root directory of the A: drive will be copied into the MAIN directory on drive C:, since you are currently logged into the MAIN directory.

The second way to copy the files into a specific directory on the C: drive is to stay in the root directory and type

COPY A:*.* C:\MAIN\[Enter]

The result is that all the files in the root directory of the A: drive are copied into the MAIN directory on drive C:. This method requires that you specify the source (A:) and destination (C: \ MAIN \) locations of the files to be copied.

The reverse is also true. If you want to copy all the .COM files from the MAIN directory on the C: drive to the A: drive, either type

COPY C: \ MAIN \ *.* A:[Enter]

or log onto the MAIN directory on the C: drive and type

COPY *.* A:[Enter]

Each command has its advantages, depending on your situation. In Chapter 7, batch files are discussed in depth. At that time, these techniques will be used to automate some common procedures.

The DATE command. This command is used to set the date in the computer. You may also use it with the AUTOEXEC.BAT file. This will be discussed in detail in Chapter 7, "Batch Files."

You might also use this command to change the date the computer uses to tag the directory. Every time you look at the directory, you'll notice that the computer shows the last time the file was modified. Maybe you want this date to be different from the actual date. For example, you might use this date as a way of keeping track of certain text files. Or you might want to make a text file look as if you worked on it when you were actually vacationing in Fiji. You can use the DATE command to change the date in the system, then open up the text file on which you want to change the date, and then save the file again. The directory will show the altered date.

To change the date, simply type

DATE[Enter]

The computer will respond with

Current date is Sat 9-19-1987
Enter new date (mm-dd-yy):

You should respond by typing the date, starting with a two-digit number for the month (such as 01 for January,

02 for February, and so on), a dash, a two-digit number
for the date (04 or 28), another dash, and the last two
digits of the year, and Enter. The date you entered will
then show as the date in all files you subsequently modify or create. Note that in version 3.3, changing the date
will make the change permanent in the internal clock on
an AT (until the next time you change it), whereas on a
PC or XT it will only make a temporary change (until the
power is turned off or the clock is changed again).

The DEL or ERASE command. The DEL and
ERASE commands (they are identical) remove a file, or
group of files, from the disk. If you want to remove a single file from the directory you are logged into, type

DEL fn.ft[Enter]

This will remove the file you specify from this directory. (Remember the naming convention mentioned in
Chapter 1: *fn.ft* stands for Filename.File Type.) If this
same filename appears in another directory, the files in
the other directory will remain unchanged. You will not
erase files in other directories unless you change directories and enter this command again.

The wildcards (* and ?) are often used in the DEL
command. For example, if you want to remove all of the
files with a file type of .BAS, type

DEL *.BAS[Enter]

The computer erases all the files with the file type of
.BAS (BASIC language program files). Please refer to
Chapter 1 for more information on wildcards. You can
also erase files on a disk other than the one on which
you are logged. For example, if you are logged onto your
hard disk and you want to erase all of the files on a
floppy disk in drive A:, you could type the command

DEL A:*.*[Enter]

This tells the computer to go to the A: drive (shown by
the A:) and erase all files matching the specified parameters. In this example, the wildcard *.* was used. This

command will erase all the files on the A: drive. If you specify all files by using the *.* option, the computer will ask if you really want to erase all the files. Note that this command will only erase the files on the currently logged directory of the drive specified. That will be the directory you were logged onto the last time you logged onto the A: drive. If there are other directories, none of the files in those directories will be erased.

The DIR command. The DIR command allows you to see what's on your disk. It will show all the files, or you can use functions called *switches* to limit the files displayed. This can be automated using batch files, which will be discussed in depth in Chapter 7. In the meantime, here's what you'll need to know to get the directory information you need.

To display a directory, type

DIR[Enter]

and the screen will display something like the following:

```
Volume in drive C: is Main Drive
Directory of C:
ANSI       SYS      1678  3-17-87  12:00p
ASSIGN     COM      1561  3-17-87  12:00p
BACKUP     COM     31913  3-18-87  12:00p
CHKDSK     COM      9850  3-18-87  12:00p
COMMAND COM        25307  3-17-87  12:00p
COMP       COM      4214  3-17-87  12:00p
FIND       EXE      6434  3-17-87  12:00p
FORMAT     COM     11616  3-18-87  12:00p
MODE       COM     15487  3-17-87  12:00p
SORT       EXE      1977  3-17-87  12:00p
TREE       COM      3571  3-17-87  12:00p
VDISK      SYS      3455  3-17-87  12:00p
12 File(s) 14196736 bytes free
```

The information displayed on the screen is a list of all the files in the directory, along with some detailed information about the files. The first column is the filename, followed by the file type. The filename can be up to eight characters long. It is followed by three characters

CHAPTER 6

which normally show the file type. The next column shows the size of the file in bytes (in the case of a text file, you can think of this as the number of characters in the file). Files can be as small as three or four characters (batch files may be this short) or as large as several million bytes.

The last two columns show the last date and time the file was modified. For example, if you make a change to a text file, or to a database information file, the date and time shown on the directory will change. This makes it very convenient to determine which version of a file is the most recent. When you use a program such as a word processor or spreadsheet, the date and time will not change. You did not change the file, you only used it.

The MKDIR or MD command. The MKDIR or MD command creates a new directory. In Chapter 3, some of the terms used below were defined, so you may want to review Chapter 3 before starting to create new directories.

If you want to create a new directory named TEST, type

```
MD TEST[Enter]
```

Note that the abbreviated MD command was used rather than MKDIR. Either will work, but most users prefer the shorthand version. If you now do a listing of the directory, you'll see a new entry called TEST, similar to this:

```
Volume in drive C: is Main Drive
Directory of C:\

TEST         <DIR>           9-24-87    1:31p
ANSI         SYS     1678    3-17-87   12:00p
ASSIGN       COM     1561    3-17-87   12:00p
BACKUP       COM    31913    3-18-87   12:00p
CHKDSK       COM     9850    3-18-87   12:00p
COMMAND      COM    25307    3-17-87   12:00p
COMP         COM     4214    3-17-87   12:00p
FIND         EXE     6434    3-17-87   12:00p
FORMAT       COM    11616    3-18-87   12:00p
MODE         COM    15487    3-17-87   12:00p
```

```
SORT      EXE      1977    3-17-87   12:00p
TREE      COM      3571    3-17-87   12:00p
VDISK     SYS      3455    3-17-87   12:00p
13 File(s) 14215168 bytes free
```

If you change directories to the TEST directory (use the CD command) and then do a listing of the directory, you will see something like

```
Volume in drive C: is Main Drive
Directory of C:\TEST

.      <DIR> 9-24-87  3:51p
..     <DIR> 9-24-87  3:51p
2 File(s) 14215168 bytes free
```

This display means that there are no files in the directory except the two entries represented by a single period and a double period. The file marked by a single period shows that you are in a directory other than the root directory. The file marked by two periods is your path to the next higher directory. If you enter

CD ..

you will go to the next higher directory. This is true of every directory except the root directory, which is the highest directory. This is discussed in more detail in the section on the CD command.

You can now add files to this directory (see COPY).

The MORE command. MORE is a pipeline command that allows you to read a screen of text before it scrolls off the screen. It is usually used in conjunction with the TYPE or DIR commands.

Let's assume you're going to look at the contents of a text file called CAT.TXT. You type

TYPE CAT.TXT I MORE[Enter]

The computer will then display the contents of the file CAT.TXT. After the screen has filled with text, it stops, and the line

— More—

appears at the bottom-left corner of the screen. Pressing any key will allow the next screen of information to be displayed.

Now assume that you need to see the contents of a directory, but it's a large directory. You can use MORE to keep the directory contents from scrolling off the screen before you have a chance to read it. To do this, type

DIR | MORE[Enter]

The computer will then display the first screen of directory information and pause, and the line

— More—

will appear at the bottom-left corner of the screen. Again, pressing any key will allow the next screen of information to be displayed before continuing.

If you plan to use this command often, read the documentation that came with your operating system for a more complete discussion.

The RMDIR or RD command. Sometimes you may have a directory that is no longer in use. The RMDIR or RD command (they are the same) will remove the unnecessary directory. The directory cannot be removed if it still contains files. If you issue the RD command and the system refuses to delete the directory, use the CD command to go to that directory, and enter DIR to make sure that there are no files left in the directory. If there are any files, copy them to another directory or disk if you want to keep them, then erase them from the directory using the DEL or ERASE command. Once the DIR command responds with the following message, there are no files left in the directory.

Volume in drive C: is Main Drive Directory of C:\TEST

```
.       <DIR>  9-24-87   3:51p
..      <DIR>  9-24-87   3:51p
2 File(s) 14215168 bytes free
```

DOS Commands

You now can go to the directory level above this one (use the CD.. command as shown in Figure 6-2) and type:

RD TEST[Enter]

The directory will then be removed.

The TIME command. This command is just like the DATE command except it deals with the time stored in the system instead of the date. You can use it to change the time, but it will lose its setting and return to the internal system clock every time you turn off the power (except in an AT). Note that, as in the case of the DATE command, if you don't have a battery-operated clock in your system, the computer will come up with an inaccurate time, and you will have to use the DATE and TIME command to set the correct information into the computer. This is discussed in more depth in Chapter 7, "Batch Files."

Note that in DOS version 3.3, changing the time will make the change permanent (until the next time you change it) in the internal clock on an AT, whereas on a PC or XT it will only make a temporary change (lasting until the power is turned off or the clock is changed again).

The TYPE command. The TYPE command allows you to display the contents of a text or ASCII file, such as one you create with a word processor. Let's assume you want to look at the contents of a text file called HOME.TXT. Type

TYPE HOME.TXT[Enter]

The computer will then display the contents of the file HOME.TXT. If the file is very long, you may want to use the MORE command previously discussed.

TYPE HOME.TXT | MORE[Enter]

Another way to stop the TYPE command from outputting text is to use the Ctrl-S key combination. This will stop the screen from scrolling and displaying any more information. To continue the scrolling, press the

Ctrl-S key again. The text will continue scrolling up the screen. If you want to cease the operation, you can press the Ctrl-C, and the TYPE command will stop.

Occasionally Used Commands

The following section lists the commands you are likely to use only once a day or less often. These commands let you back up your files to another disk, verify the integrity of your disk, clear the screen, set the path where DOS looks for files, format a disk, set the mode of the system, recover erased files, and rename files.

The BACKUP and RESTORE commands. The BACKUP command copies the files from your hard disk to floppy disks in a special compacted format. The RESTORE command can then restore the proper operation of the hard disk in the event of a failure.

Hard disks are usually reliable, offering years of operation before they exhibit signs of wear or failure. However, almost any user of a computer with a hard disk can tell you at least one horror story about hours, days, weeks, or even years of work lost. Many of those tragedies could have been avoided if those users had backed up the files on their hard disks.

Obviously, the RESTORE command can only restore files that you have dutifully backed up to floppies, so the more often you use these two commands, the safer you are. Also, never rely on your backup as being fail-safe. The floppy you back up to can also be bad. Doubling backup for very valuable files is always a good idea. The general rule of thumb is to back up as often as you feel you need to, keeping in mind how much work you can afford to lose. A professional writer should use BACKUP at least once a day.

The general syntax of the BACKUP command is:

BACKUP source destination[Enter]

The word *source* refers to the group of files to be backed up, and *destination* is the disk where the backup files are to be stored.

DOS Commands

The general syntax of the RESTORE command is:

`RESTORE source destination[Enter]`

Here *source* refers to the group of files stored as backup files. The word *destination* tells DOS where the backup files should be put.

The BACKUP and RESTORE commands are quite complex. Only the general procedure for using them is shown here. If you want to use BACKUP and RESTORE with all their possible features, refer to your DOS manual for a full description.

A note for users of DOS 3.3: Version 3.3 now allows you to backup files selectively, based on selection by date or time, and it allows you to backup to floppy disks that have not been formatted. It formats them during the backup process.

The CHKDSK command. The CHKDSK command allows you to determine the integrity of a disk, and it tells you how much space is being used on the disk and how much is free. This command can be used on either hard or floppy disks. Type

`CHKDSK`

You will be provided with a report similar to the following:

```
Volume Main Drive created Oct 24, 1987 3:52p

21309440    bytes total disk space
   53248    bytes in 3 hidden files
   38912    bytes in 16 directories
11520000    bytes in 395 user files
 9627648    bytes available on disk

  655360    bytes total memory
  449808    bytes free
```

If you have any errors on your disk, CHKDSK will notify you of the errors.

To tell CHKDSK to attempt to fix any errors it finds in the directory or the file allocation table, type

`CHKDSK /F`

(The file allocation table is a part of the disk that tells the directory where the files are located.)

To tell CHKDSK to display all files and their paths, type

CHKDSK /V

To tell CHKDSK to display the results of its operation on a file (in this case file *fn.ft* located on the B: drive) type

CHKDSK B:fn.ft

The CHKDSK command also recognizes path and filename parameters. For more information, refer to the DOS manual that came with your system.

The CLS command. The CLS command clears the screen. This is most often used with batch files to clear the screen after some operation that leaves the screen cluttered. You might also consider it a security tool, since by running it after every application you will always leave a clean screen, and confidential information that appeared on the screen will have been removed. CLS is also discussed in Chapter 7, "Batch Files."

The FORMAT command. The FORMAT command allows you to format a disk, removing all the previous information from the disk to prepare it for fresh data. The FORMAT command also allows you to copy DOS to the disk.

You should exercise extreme caution with the format command. The FORMAT command also allows you to reformat your hard disk. If that happens, you will lose all the information you have stored there. (Actually, you may be able to retrieve the information, through the use of special programs. But it would be better not to lose it in the first place.)

FORMAT has many switches to allow you to control how a disk is formatted. If you need any advanced formatting information, refer to your DOS manual. Most of the time all you will be doing is formatting floppy disks.

Let's assume that the disk you are going to format is in drive A: and you are logged onto drive C:. To format the disk in drive A:, type

FORMAT A:[Enter]

DOS will display the following message:

Insert new diskette for drive A:
and strike ENTER when ready

You should insert the disk to be formatted in drive A: and press the Enter key. When the format process is finished, DOS will display the message:

Format complete

\<x\> bytes total disk space
\<x\> bytes used by system
\<x\> bytes available on disk

Format another (Y/N)?

If you answer with a Y, DOS will display instructions for repeating the process. If you answer N, DOS will return you to the C: prompt.

If you want to create a disk with DOS on it, so that you can start your computer from it, you need to have DOS copied to the disk. This cannot be done with the COPY command, as there are two hidden files that need to be transferred.

To format a disk with DOS on it, type

FORMAT A:/S[Enter]

DOS will prompt you to insert your DOS disk. When your computer is done reading it, you will see the following message:

Insert new diskette for drive A:
and strike ENTER when ready

You should insert the disk to be formatted in drive A: and press the Enter key. When the format process is finished, and a copy of DOS has been transferred to the disk, DOS will display the message:

```
Format complete
System Transferred
```

```
<x> bytes total disk space
<x> bytes used by system
<x> bytes available on disk
```

```
Format another (Y/N)?
```

Your disk is now formatted, is ready for use, and contains the two hidden DOS files as well as the file COMMAND.COM.

The MODE command. Another of the complex commands in DOS, MODE sets up the video adapter (such as a monochrome, CGA, or EGA system), sets up the parameters of the serial port (COM1:, for example), redirects printer assignments from the default printer port (LPT1:) to any of the other possible ports, and does more. This allows you have the computer to talk to more than one printer by having several printers connected to the computer and using the MODE command to switch among the ports.

For example, you may have a dot-matrix printer connected to the parallel port and a laser printer connected to a serial port. Using a batch file, you can tell the computer which printer to send your file to, and the batch file will execute all the necessary commands. The following section describes some of the functions and uses of the MODE command. If you need more information, refer to the DOS manuals that came with your computer system.

Video functions. Let's look at the video functions first. Your computer may have more than one video card installed. For example, you might have a monochrome card for text display, but switch to a CGA card to run games. Of course, this means that you probably have two monitors, but the computer and DOS can handle both of them without any problem. If you are doing word processing, and you wanted all of your displays to be on the monochrome monitor, you could use the command

```
MODE MONO[Enter]
```

This command will cause all output to be displayed on
the monochrome screen through the monochrome video
card. Now let's say that you are through with your writing for the day and want to play a game in color. You
need to switch to the other monitor. You do this with the
command

MODE CO80

which will switch all output to the color monitor. Naturally, the programs themselves must also be configured
for the proper screen.

   Two of the same type of video display cards cannot
normally be plugged into the system. If you are trying to
combine video display cards of different types, read the
manuals carefully, since monochrome and color cards use
different areas of the computer's memory for their display. A monochrome card uses only a small part so will
not usually interfere with the operation of a color display.
Two color displays, however, will almost always use the
same area of the computer's memory, and the resulting
interference will cause the combination to fail. There are
ways to get around this problem, though it is far beyond
the scope of this book. It involves remapping the video
display memory, which can only be done if one of the
cards is an EGA card, since they have their own BIOS
ROM (which must be modified). If this sounds like a lot
of work, you're right. It is something better left to professional programmers and developers.

   Modem functions. Let's look at the MODE command
and see how to get it to work with some of your printers
or modems. Let's say you are hooking up a modem to
port 1, usually called COM1.

   In another application, you may need to set the parameters for output from the serial port, COM1. The
command

MODE COM1:1200,N,8,1

will set port 1 up for 1200 baud, no parity, eight data
bits, and one stop bit. This is a normal configuration for a

1200-baud modem when you are using the modem to communicate with another computer or a bulletin board system.

Note that you may not have to run this program, since many telecommunications programs have functions in them (some automatic) that set up the port for you. If you are not sure, use the line above to set up the port; then use the modem and a communications program to get into a bulletin board system. Next, repeat the line above, but substitute something like 9600 for the 1200, thus changing the baud rate to something that the bulletin board and your modem probably can't use. Run the communications program again. If you successfully establish communications with the bulletin board, your program initialized the port, and the MODE command does not need to be run. If you can't establish communications, try running the MODE command again, this time using the 1200 value, then establish communications with the bulletin board. If you succeed, you will know that you have to run the MODE command each time you use the modem. If you are still unable to establish contact, you are probably doing something wrong with the communications program, and you will need to go back and read your manual.

Printer functions. You might also use a serial port to connect the computer to a printer. To do this, you will probably need to initialize the printer port, in this case shown as COM2 (port 2), to match the printer. Check with your printer manual to determine what settings are required for the printer. Some printers are equipped with small switches to set the parameters. If yours is one of these, you should make sure you are adjusting both the computer and the printer to the same settings. In the following example, you'll use the values of 9600 baud, no parity, eight data bits, and one stop bit.

Once your printer is set to these values, you can type the following command line to set the computer to the same values:

MODE COM2:9600,N,8,1,P

These values will set the port COM2 to 9600 baud, no parity, eight data bits, one stop bit, and specify that the data is to be sent to a printer. If your printer has different settings, make sure that you make corresponding changes to the MODE command. The computer also needs to be told that the printer is connected to a serial port, since it expects to find the printer on a parallel port. This is called the *default printer port,* and if your printer is connected to a port other than LPT1 (parallel printer port 1), you will need to tell the computer where to find the printer. The command

MODE LPT1:=COM2:

will send information normally sent to the default printer port (usually the first parallel port) to the serial port.

There are many other possible combinations that can be set up using the MODE command. If you need to use the MODE command, you should refer to the proper section of your DOS manual, and to your computer manual, to find out which ports and display options you have in your computer and what functions you can change using the MODE command.

The PATH command. The PATH command allows you to set the path through the directory structure where DOS will search for a program. For example, you might have your word processing program in a directory called WORDPROC, your spreadsheet program in a directory called SPREAD, and your utilities in a directory called UTILITY. Normally, to use these programs, you would have to go to the directory where the program is located to run the program. This can become inconvenient at times, especially if some of the utilities located in the UTILITY directory are used with files in both the WORDPROC and SPREAD directories.

The PATH command is normally made a part of the AUTOEXEC.BAT file, and is covered with examples in Chapter 11.

The RECOVER command. This command is used in conjunction with the BACKUP command and is discussed there.

The REN or RENAME command. The REN or RE-
NAME command (they are the same) changes the name
of a specified file. For example, let's assume you have a
file, AUTOEXEC.BAT, and you want to create another
one, but don't want to wipe out the old one. The solution
is to rename the old one, then create the new one. This is
simply done by typing

REN AUTOEXEC.BAT AUTOBACK.BAT[Enter]

This will rename the file AUTOEXEC.BAT to AUTO-
BACK.BAT. The REN command is followed first by the
file that is to be changed, then by the filename to which
it should be changed.

Seldom Used Commands

The following sections list commands that you are un-
likely to use, or commands that you will use rarely. Since
this book is designed to get you going with DOS, not to
make you a power user, the following sections are brief.
If you need more information about a command, you
should refer to your DOS manual.

The APPEND command. This command provides a
function similar to the PATH command in that it allows
DOS to locate files outside the current directory. The
PATH command is limited to file types .COM, .EXE, and
.BAT, where the APPEND command can locate files of
any extension type. APPEND is not a substitute for the
PATH command, but is used with it. Note that the AP-
PEND command for earlier versions of DOS was slow,
but the speed of APPEND for DOS 3.3 has been
improved.

The ASSIGN command. This command tells DOS to
route disk instructions to a different drive than the one
specified. For example, if you type

ASSIGN A=B[Enter]

then a DIR A: command will display the contents of drive
B:.

DOS Commands

The ATTRIB command. This command sets the attributes for files. Each file in the directory has certain attributes, such as Read Only or Archive, which you may want to change. The ATTRIB command allows you to make these changes. Note that in DOS 3.3 a new switch, /S, has been added to allow ATTRIB to affect the specified directory and all subdirectories.

The BREAK command. This command allows you to tell DOS when to check for a Ctrl-Break condition, sometimes used where you may want to break into the operation of the program. By typing

```
BREAK ON
```

you will cause DOS to respond to a Ctrl-Break whenever it is requested. By typing

```
BREAK OFF
```

you will cause DOS to check for a Ctrl-Break only during standard input/output operations. Input/output operations (also called *I/O operations* or just *I/O*) are operations in which the computer receives or sends information to an external device. Printing text on the screen and receiving information from the keyboard are examples of I/O operations.

The CHCP command. This command selects the code page that DOS uses for changing screen display characters. This is normally only used in countries outside the United States. This command is new with version 3.3.

The COMMAND command. This command starts a secondary command processor. This command is used only by advanced users to change command processors for special functions.

The COMP command. This command compares the contents of two files. The syntax is

```
COMP File1 File2[Enter]
```

The variables File1 and File2 stand for the names of the two files to be compared. If the files match, the computer will display the message

Files compare OK

which means the files are identical (though the names
may be different). If the files are different, the computer
will display a message telling the offset at which the difference occurred.

The CTTY command. This command changes the
standard console (keyboard and display) to another device. These alternate devices may be AUX, COM1,
COM2, COM3, or COM4. If you want to change the console to the COM1 port, type

CTTY COM1[Enter]

To return to the standard console, you type

CTTY CON[Enter]

The DISKCOMP command. This command compares the contents of two disks (it will not work on a
hard disk.) The syntax is

DISKCOMP disk1 disk2[Enter]

where *disk1* and *disk2* stand for the names of the two
disks to be compared. If the disks are identical,
DISKCOMP will display the message

Diskettes compare OK

If the disks are different, DISKCOMP will display the
message

Compare error

Disks made with the COPY command may not compare even though the directories show the same files.
This is because the computer placed the files on the disk
in a different order, even though the directories are identical. DISKCOMP is normally used to verify disk copies
made with the DISKCOPY command (see below).

The DISKCOPY command. The DISKCOPY com-
mand copies a disk. The copies are identical to the original, and DISKCOPY will format the destination disk if

necessary. DISKCOPY will not always make an accurate copy of software that is copy-protected. The syntax is

DISKCOPY source destination

Here *source* is the disk you want to copy, and *destination* is the disk to which the files are to be copied.

The EXE2BIN command. This command is no longer included with 3.3, but is supplied with the *DOS 3.3 Technical Reference Manual* from IBM.

The FASTOPEN command. The FASTOPEN command allows you to access files in your directories faster by storing the location of the disk files in the computer's memory. This allows the computer to know the location of the files without having to read the disk directory every time it reads from a file. The FASTOPEN command is normally only used on systems with hard disks, and it's normally run by the AUTOEXEC.BAT file when the system is turned on. This is a new command for version 3.3.

The FDISK command. The FDISK command is used to set up your hard disk. It is normally run only once—when setting up the hard disk or adding another hard disk. If you need to use this command, refer to the manuals that came with your hard disk or refer to your DOS manual.

The FIND command. This command (filter) is used to display (or print) all lines in a file, or group of files, that contain a specified string of characters. This is normally only used by programmers to find routines in programs they have written.

The GRAFTABL command. This command loads a table of additional character data into memory for color or graphics mode. This is used, for example, to display international language characters or graphics characters on the screen.

The GRAPHICS command. This command allows the screen display to be printed on an IBM printer (or a compatible printer) when using a CGA display adapter.

CHAPTER 6

The JOIN command. The JOIN command allows you to join two directories, on two separate drives, to form a single directory.

The KEYB command. This command loads a program that allows you to use non-English keyboards.

The LABEL command. This command allows you to add, delete, or change the volume label on a disk. The volume label is an 11-character name that appears at the top of every directory listing.

The NLSFUNC command. This is a new command for version 3.3. It supports additional screen display characters along with the CHCP command.

The PROMPT command. The system prompt is the character that you see on the screen, such as A> or C>, that indicates the computer is ready to receive a command. The PROMPT command allows you to change the system prompt to provide additional information. This is normally run from the AUTOEXEC.BAT file, though you can use it to change the prompt at any time. For example, if you want the prompt to display the directory you are logged into, type the line

```
PROMPT $P$G[Enter]
```

When you are in the root directory, the prompt will be

```
<C:\>
```

The \ character indicates you are in the ROOT directory. When you move, for example, to a directory named MAIN, the prompt will be

```
C:\MAIN>
```

The $P in the example above told DOS to display the current directory; the $G told DOS to display the prompt character. The following list shows some of the characters that can be used to make the prompt display information.

Character   **Information Displayed at Prompt**
  T   Time
  D   Date
  P   Directory
  V   DOS version number
  N   Drive letter
  G   The > character
  L   The < character
  B   The | character
  Q   The = character
  H   Backspace, erases the previous character
  E   The ESCape character
  _   CR/LF, moves the prompt to the next line

More information on the PROMPT command is provided in Chapter 11.

The REPLACE command. The REPLACE command is an enhanced version of the COPY command that allows you to replace files on one disk with files from another disk. The REPLACE command is normally used when upgrading your version of DOS, or sometimes it may be used when you are upgrading to a later version of an applications software package.

The SELECT command. The SELECT command installs DOS on a new disk and allows you to define the country code and keyboard layout. This command formats the disk, copies the DOS files to the new disk, then creates a predefined AUTOEXEC.BAT file and CONFIG.SYS file on the new disk.

The SET command. The SET command displays or sets the command processor's environment. This is a complex command for advanced users only.

The SHARE command. The SHARE command provides file sharing support for systems with more than one user.

The SORT command. The SORT command is a filter that takes data from a file, sorts it, and outputs the data to another file. In addition, it can sort a screen display. This sort function is quite limited. If you need to do extensive sorting, you should investigate some of the sort programs available in other commercial packages or in public domain software.

The SUBST command. The SUBST command allows you to substitute a drive letter for a path. For example, a subdirectory that is several levels removed from the root directory (such as ARCHIVE in Figure 6-2) can be called as a drive (drive D:, for example) rather than specifying the path (WORDPROC \ ARCHIVE) to that subdirectory. Thus, the command

SUBST D: C: \ WORDPROC \ ARCHIVE[Enter]

will substitute the ARCHIVE subdirectory for the drive D:. You can then type

DIR D:[Enter]

to display the directory of the ARCHIVE subdirectory, instead of having to type the entire WORDPROC \ ARCHIVE path. If you specify a drive greater than the LASTDRIVE value in your CONFIG.SYS file, SUBST will not work. The default last drive is E:, which means that you cannot have a drive with a letter later in the alphabet than *E* unless you alter your CONFIG.SYS file.

The SYS command. The SYS command copies the two hidden DOS files onto a disk. This command only works for disks where space has been left for DOS, but where DOS was not included. This is sometimes the case with applications programs. If space has not been left on the disk for DOS (as is the case when you use the FORMAT command without the /S option), SYS will not copy the system. Normally you would use the /S option of the FORMAT command to copy DOS to a disk, though this also formats the disk.

DOS Commands

The TREE command. This command lists the directories on the disk.

The VER command. The VER command tells you which version of the operating system is being used. If you type

VER[Enter]

the computer will respond with a message similar to

IBM Personal Computer DOS Version 3.30

The VERIFY command. The VERIFY command causes DOS to verify the integrity of data after writing it to a disk. Because of the time it takes for DOS to reread the data after every write to disk, this command is rarely used except where the disk is suspected of being bad. If you think a disk is bad, you would be well advised to dispose of it.

The VOL command. This command displays the volume label on a disk. The volume label is an 11-character name that appears at the top of every directory listing. It's written to the disk by the FORMAT or LABEL commands.

The XCOPY command. The XCOPY command allows you to copy a file or group of files selectively.

Chapter 7
Batch Files

Chapter 7

Batch Files

This chapter discusses the batch commands used in batch files. Batch files are essentially a combination of a program you write and act as a substitute for the keyboard. The file contains lines typed as if you had typed them from the keyboard. The batch file is, therefore, a shorthand way to "type" large strings of keyboard commands by typing only a single command. The first step in using a batch file is to create it.

As an example, to create a batch file that will display a directory of all your BASIC files, you could create a batch file called BAS.BAT that contains the line

DIR *.BAS

The easiest way to do this is by typing the following:

COPY CON BAS.BAT[Enter]
DIR *.BAS[Ctrl-Z][Enter]

The computer should respond with the following message:

1 file(s) copied

Let's look at what you did. When you typed the line COPY CON BAS.BAT, you told the computer to COPY what you typed on the CONsole (your keyboard) into a file called BAS.BAT. You then typed DIR *.BAS, followed by Ctrl-Z and Enter, and the computer entered this line into the file. The Ctrl-Z told the computer that this would be the end of the file, and when you pressed Enter, it saved the file on the computer's disk. This process created a program called BAS.BAT.

CHAPTER 7

Remember that entering a Ctrl-Z is done by pressing the Ctrl key and holding it while you type the letter Z. You don't have to press the shift key—either upper- or lowercase will do.

To run the program, type

BAS[Enter]

When the program runs, the batch file will type the keyboard input for you. In this case, it types the line

DIR *.BAS

as if it were coming from your keyboard.

All batch files work in this manner by saving the command lines in a file and typing them for you when you run the batch file.

Batch files can be quite complex. Some have been created with several thousand lines in them. These are usually created with an editor such as EDLIN (the editor that comes with DOS) or *WordStar* (in nondocument mode).

Batch files can use virtually all of the commands normally found and used in any DOS operation, as well as the commands used to execute any of your normal application programs such as word processing programs, spreadsheets, or databases. In addition, there are some commands that are normally used only by batch files. All of these commands are discussed briefly in the following paragraphs. If you need more extensive information for these commands, you should refer to the detailed information in your DOS manuals. Chapter 12 deals with using batch files in the operation of DOS.

The CALL command. The CALL command is a new command for version 3.3. The CALL command allows you to use another batch file without ending the batch file being executed. Normally, when you are running a batch file, if it calls another batch file, the original batch file is terminated. By using the CALL command, you can run another batch file, and when the second one is completed, control will return to the first batch file. The following is an example of one batch file calling another and then returning to finish executing the original batch file. This file is called CLEANUP.BAT.

```
DIR *.BAK
CALL ERABAK
DIR *.BAK
```

The following file is the batch file called by CLEANUP.BAT. It's called ERABAK.BAT.

```
ERASE *.BAK
```

If you save these batch files with the names provided and then type CLEANUP, the batch file CLEANUP.BAT will first display a listing of the files in the directory with a file type of .BAK. These are backup files, usually found in word processing applications. It will then call the batch file ERABAK.BAT which will erase all of the files with a file type of .BAK. Control returns to the batch program CLEANUP.BAT, which will try to display a listing of the .BAK files in the directory. Since there now should be none, the screen should display the following message:

```
File not found
```

The ECHO command. The ECHO command allows, or prevents, the screen from displaying the DOS commands as they are executed from a batch file. For example, if your batch file had the line

```
ECHO OFF
```

the commands sent by the batch file would not be displayed.

The FOR IN DO command. The FOR IN DO command allows a batch command to repeat itself. The syntax of the command is

```
FOR n IN files DO command
```

where *n* is the number of times the command is to be repeated, *files* is the list of files to be acted upon, and *command* is the action to be taken on the files. For example:

```
FOR %%A IN (*.BAT) DO TYPE %%A
```

would type a continuous listing of all the .BAT files in the directory.

The GOTO command. The GOTO command causes the batch file to jump to the line in the batch file containing the indicated label. For example:

GOTO TEST

would cause the batch file to jump from the line containing the GOTO command to the line with the label TEST, skipping any lines in between.

The IF [NOT] command. The IF [NOT] command allows the batch file to jump to a line, similar to the GOTO command, but only if a condition is met. For example, if the batch file has the line

IF EXIST fn.ft GOTO TEST

the batch file would go to the line labeled TEST only if the file *fn.ft* existed on the directory. If the file didn't exist, the batch file would continue processing the next command. This is covered further in Chapter 12.

The PAUSE command. The PAUSE command causes the batch file to stop running and displays the message

Strike a key when ready. . . .

This allows you to put messages in your batch file and causes the computer to pause so you can read them. Once you have read the instruction, press a key and the batch file will continue processing.

The REM command. The REM command allows you to insert lines in the batch file to help document what you have done. After you have been programming for a period of time, you will find that more and more of your programming time is spent updating and adapting programs. When you sit down to correct a program of more than a dozen lines, you may have trouble identifying the purpose of certain routines and commands. Documenting the batch file will be a great help to you when your return to do some correcting and updating.

The SHIFT command. Batch files often require parameters. A parameter might tell the program what file to act on, for instance, or what routines to run. Normally you are limited to ten parameters, but using the SHIFT command allows you to have more than ten. That is beyond the scope of this book.

Chapter 8

The CONFIG.SYS File

Chapter 8

The CONFIG.SYS File

When you first turn on your computer, it goes to ROM (Read-Only Memory) in the computer. Normally this memory tells the computer to go to a disk, either a floppy or a hard disk, and load DOS. Part of DOS is a file called CONFIG.SYS.

This file is optional. Your system will work without it, but using it allows you to add many additional functions. This file sets up the computer to use the date and time conventions of a specified country, adds buffers and reserves memory for certain functions, defines the way the computer retrieves files from the disks, and has other functions.

The following sections discuss each of these items, and at the end of the chapter a sample CONFIG.SYS is provided. The sample CONFIG.SYS includes modification procedures so you can modify it for your particular requirements. Remember that this is a book for beginners. Don't expect great detail in the discussion to follow. The manuals that came with your DOS discuss the more complex functions in detail.

Commands

The CONFIG.SYS file contains a number of command lines, and may look like the following:

```
DEVICE = ANSI.SYS
BUFFERS = 20
FILES = 20
```

Of course, it may not contain these lines. Or it may have these and many more lines. Each of these commands, such as DEVICE, BUFFERS, and FILES as shown above, provide your computer with additional capabilities.

Let's look at each of the possible commands first, and then look at a sample CONFIG.SYS file at the end of the chapter.

The BREAK command. There are times where you may want to break into the operation of the program. Pressing the Ctrl and Break keys simultaneously usually does this, but not always. Some programs, such as compilers, may turn off this ability before they run. By inserting the command BREAK = ON into the CONFIG.SYS file, you can override the program, break into the execution, and halt it. The normal configuration is BREAK = OFF, and the computer will assume this condition if you make no entry in your CONFIG.SYS file. Interrupting the operation of some programs can cause damage to the program. Unless you have experience in operation of your programs and are aware of the risks, I suggest you not use the BREAK command in your CONFIG.SYS file.

The BUFFERS command. Buffers are an area in the computer's memory where information moving to or from a disk is stored before it is used. The BUFFER command allows you to set the number of buffers in memory to a value different from its default value. Buffers can make the computer operate more quickly, since DOS checks to see if it has already loaded the information into a buffer before going to the disk for it. This will often be the case in word processing programs, databases, and graphics programs.

If the information is already in the buffer, DOS will move it directly to the program without going to the disk. Thus, since the computer can access its own memory many times faster than it can access a disk, the operation of the computer becomes much faster. The more that's moved into the buffer area, the faster the system will run. There is a tradeoff, however. The more space in memory set up as a buffer area, the less space there is for programs.

DOS (version 3.3) automatically sets up buffer sizes based on the following information.

System Configuration	Number of Buffers
Basic PC	2
High-Capacity Drives	3
Over 128K of memory	5
Over 256K of memory	10
Over 512K of memory	15

You can always set the number of buffers to be more or less than the number shown above. If you are using a program such as *Lotus 1-2-3* or a word processor such as *WordStar* 4.0, and you have 640K of memory, you may want to set the buffers to 20 or 25 for increased performance. Note that the above table applies only to version 3.3. Earlier versions of DOS always set the number of buffers to 2.

The COUNTRY command. The country code specifies the format of date, time, sorting sequence, capitalization, currency symbols, and comma/decimal usage. Note that this function does NOT provide any form of language translation.

Normally, the only time the COUNTRY command is used is when the computer is located in or is used in a country other than the United States, or if the code page option (new to version 3.3) is used.

The DEVICE command. The DEVICE command allows you to add device drivers to your system. For example, if you are using a mouse, your CONFIG.SYS file will contain a line similar to

```
DEVICE = MOUSE /C1
```

This tells the system that an additional piece of software is to be added to the operating system that allows your mouse to work with DOS.

Another use for the DEVICE command is to add some types of ramdisk drives (the VDISK.SYS command can also perform this function). Software packages that add ramdisks provide complete installation instructions. You will need to refer to them, as each package is different.

Device drivers. DOS includes files called *device drivers* (used with the DEVICE command). These files are identified with a file type of .SYS, and must be located in the ROOT directory. Usually, the use of these files will be dependent on the software you are running.

A device driver is like an addition to the DOS operating system. It adds a function or capability not originally included with the operating system, or it modifies the operating system so that it performs certain functions differently as required by your particular software. Your application software manuals will discuss which device drivers you should use. A brief summary of the device drivers normally included with DOS follows.

ANSI.SYS. This driver is used to provide extended screen and keyboard control. This may be used when a different type of display is used (for example, some large display screens), or a different type of keyboard is used that may affect the character set.

DISPLAY.SYS. This driver allows you to use code page-switching on the PC convertible, EGA systems, and Personal System/2 displays. It's unusual for most users to need this driver. If you need it, your applications software manuals will tell you how to use it.

DRIVER.SYS. This driver allows you to use a disk device through the use of a logical drive letter. Normally you will not need to use this driver unless your specific application package requires it. In that case, the manual will detail what you need to put in the command line to use the driver.

PRINTER.SYS. This driver provides code page-switching with the IBM Proprinter Model 4201 and IBM Quietwriter III Model 5202. Normally, a United States user will not need to use this driver. If you are a foreign

The CONFIG.SYS File

user, the DOS manual details the information you need.

VDISK.SYS. This driver allows you to use part of your computer memory as a simulated disk drive called a *ramdisk* or a *virtual disk*.

Using a virtual disk will make your system operate much more quickly because it doesn't have to wait for a slow mechanical device to read information from a disk. The idea is to set aside part of the computer memory as a disk drive, then to store in it information you access often, such as a dictionary. From that time on, each time you access the information, the computer will only have to go to its own memory instead of going out to the relatively slow disk drive.

A disadvantage of a virtual disk is that each time the power is turned off, the memory in the virtual disk is lost. You have two choices. Either copy the information from the virtual disk to the computer's real disk drives (an ideal application for a batch file which I'll cover later), or don't place information on the ramdisk that you can't afford to lose.

As mentioned above, spelling checker dictionaries are an ideal application for ramdisks. A simple batch file could copy the dictionary to the ramdisk every time the computer is turned on, or the batch file might load it when you call the word processor.

Remember that when a file is loaded from a disk into a ramdisk, the original is not lost, it's merely copied.

An example of a line in the CONFIG.SYS file which installs a virtual disk would be

```
DEVICE = VDISK.SYS 160 512 64
```

This command will install a 160K ramdisk, using 512-byte sectors and allowing 64 directory entries. Assuming you have a computer with two floppy disks, drives A: and B:, and a hard disk, drive C:, this driver will automatically install the virtual disk as drive D:. The driver also allows you to use extended memory (memory that is located above the 1MB boundary.) If you have this memory available, refer to the manual that came with your ex-

93

tended memory card to see how to configure it as a
ramdisk.

The FCBS command. The FCBS command allows
you to control the number of file control blocks that can
be open at any time. Usually this command is used in
applications using file sharing. For a single-user system,
file block sharing is not normally an issue, so this command is not used. When you are using a system as a file
server, or when you may have many files open at once,
as may happen with databases, your applications software manuals will tell you how to set up the FCBS
command.

The FILES command. This command allows you to
specify the number of files that can be open at the same
time. Normally DOS allows 8 files to be open at any one
time; however the FILES command allows you to have
up to 255 files open at any time. Certain databases may
require a greater number of files to be open at the same
time. Your system will usually issue an error message if
there is a problem. If you get an error message, your
applications software manuals should tell you how to set
up the FILES command.

The LASTDRIVE command. This command was referred to under the DOS command SUBST. You are only
allowed five drives according to the DOS default, lettered
A: through *E:*. You may change this, simply by entering a
line like the following in your CONFIG.SYS file:

`LASTDRIVE = G`

If you have a system with only two floppy drives,
you may want to limit access to drives A: and B:. If you
set LASTDRIVE to less than the actual number in the system, the computer will ignore the LASTDRIVE command.

The SHELL command. This command allows you to
tell DOS to use an alternative command processor that
DOS will load and use in place of COMMAND.COM.
One possibility might be a menu program that allows you
to select which program you wish to run from a menu on
the screen instead of having to type in the name of the

program. There are a number of programs like this on the market, and they often make the operation of the computer friendlier and simpler. The instructions that come with the command processor will tell you how to go about using this command for their specific program.

The STACK command. The STACK command allows you to redefine the stack parameters. This command would only used by advanced programmers.

Sample CONFIG.SYS File

The following shows a sample CONFIG.SYS file:

```
DEVICE = ANSI.SYS
DEVICE = VDISK.SYS 160 512 64
DEVICE = MSMOUSE.SYS
BUFFERS = 20
FILES = 20
```

The first line installs a driver, ANSI.SYS, that extends the capability of DOS in handling the keyboard and display. The second line installs a ramdisk. Using this command would allow you to alter your AUTOEXEC.BAT file to call a batch file that transfers frequently used files to the ramdisk for execution.

The third line installs a mouse driver, MSMOUSE.SYS, that allows the use of a mouse with certain programs. Some desktop publishing and drawing programs require this driver. The fourth and fifth lines set up the number of disk buffers to open and define the number of files that can be open at any one time.

The CONFIG.SYS file is easily created using an editor, such as EDLIN, or it can be created by using the COPY CON *fn.ft* command. This is done by typing the lines below. Before typing them, however, you should put a formatted disk in the disk drive that is different from the disk used to start the computer. The reason is that when you are through typing, the file will be saved on the disk and will write over your old CONFIG.SYS file. Change disks (unless you really want to replace your existing CONFIG.SYS disk and you aren't concerned about entering a typographical error) and enter the following lines as they are written:

```
COPY CON CONFIG.SYS[Enter]
DEVICE = ANSI.SYS[Enter]
DEVICE = VDISK.SYS 160 512 64[Enter]
DEVICE = MSMOUSE.SYS[Enter]
BUFFERS = 20[Enter]
FILES = 20[Ctrl-Z][Enter]
```

The computer should respond with the following message:

```
1 file(s) copied
```

This is similar to what was shown at the beginning of Chapter 7, "Batch Files." When you typed the line

```
COPY CON CONFIG.SYS
```

you told the computer to COPY what you type on the CONsole (your keyboard) into a file called CONFIG.SYS. You then typed the five lines of the CONFIG.SYS file, then pressed a Ctrl-Z. The Ctrl-Z told the computer that this would be the end of the file. Then you pressed Enter. The computer entered these lines into a file and saved the file.

Remember that entering a Ctrl-Z is done by pressing the Ctrl key and holding it while you type the letter Z. You don't have to press the shift key, either upper- or lowercase will work.

Once again, please note that when creating files in this manner the computer doesn't check to see if the file already exists on the disk. If one does, it overwrites the old file, which will be lost.

Chapter 9

Using EDLIN

Chapter 9

Using EDLIN

EDLIN is an editing program that allows you to create and edit text files such as the CONFIG.SYS file, the AUTOEXEC.BAT file, and any other batch file. It is a line-oriented editor, meaning that it does not have any of the refined capabilities of even the most basic word processor. What it does have to offer is ease of use, and it comes free with DOS.

Since EDLIN has no word processing capabilities, if you plan to do any serious word processing, you should obtain and use one of the popular word processing packages available. There are many, ranging in price from $500.00 to free.

This chapter will list the EDLIN commands and show you how to use them when creating the batch files discussed elsewhere in this book. This chapter is intended to give you an idea of what EDLIN can do, not to be a complete course in its use. If you plan to use EDLIN as your regular editor, refer to your DOS manuals for additional information.

Starting EDLIN

When starting EDLIN, the normal procedure is to type

```
EDLIN fn.ft[Enter]
```

The variable *fn.ft* stands for the name of the file you want to edit. For example, to edit the AUTOEXEC.BAT file, you would type

```
EDLIN AUTOEXEC.BAT[Enter]
```

EDLIN will load the file and display an asterisk prompt, indicating it is ready for a command.

EDLIN Commands

The following sections list each of the commands.

A (Append). The Append command opens a disk file and takes from it the number of lines specified in the command. These lines are then appended to the end of the file currently in memory. This command is normally required only when the file being edited is too large to fit in memory at once, and EDLIN must edit the file in pieces. The syntax is

`<x>A`

where <x> represents the number of lines from the file on disk you want to append to the file in memory.

C (Copy). The Copy command copies a group of lines to another location. The syntax is

`first,last,where,count C`

The variables *first* and *last* are the first and last line numbers of the block to be copied. The variable *where* is the line number in front of which you want to insert the copy. The variable *count* is the number of times the block should be copied.

D (Delete Line). The Delete Line command deletes a line or group of lines. The syntax is

`first,last D`

The variables *first* and *last* are the first and last line numbers of the block to be deleted.

E (End). The End command saves the file you are editing and quits EDLIN.

I (Insert). The Insert command inserts a line between two existing lines. The syntax is

`<x>I`

where <x> represents the line number before which

EDLIN is to insert a line. For example, if you want to insert a line between lines 5 and 6, you would type

6I[Enter]

EDLIN stays in the insert mode until you press the Ctrl-C or the Ctrl-Break key combination.

L (List). The List command lists a selected group of lines in the file. The syntax is

first,last L

The variables *first* and *last* are the first and last line numbers of the block to be listed.

M (Move). The Move command moves a group of lines to another location. The syntax is

first,last,where M

The variables *first* and *last* are the first and last line numbers of the block to be moved. The variable *where* is the line number in front of which you want to move the lines.

P (Page). The Page command pages through a selected group of lines in the file, listing them on the screen 23 lines at a time. The syntax is

first,last P

The variables *first* and *last* are the first and last line numbers of the block to be listed.

Q (Quit). The Quit command exits EDLIN without saving the changes you have made.

R (Replace). The Replace command replaces all occurrences of a group of characters with another group of characters. The syntax is

<x>,<x>R from[F6]to

where <x>,<x> are the first and last line numbers of the block to be scanned, and the F6 key separates the *from* and *to* groups of characters.

CHAPTER 9

S (Search). The Search command looks for a specified group of characters. The syntax is

```
<x>,<x>S search string
```

where <x>,<x> are the first and last line numbers of the block to be scanned, and *search string* is the group of characters you are looking for.

T (Transfer). The Transfer command inserts a file on disk into the file you are editing. The syntax is

```
<x>T fn.ft
```

T inserts the specified file before the line specified by <x>, and *fn.ft* specifies the file to be inserted.

W (Write). The Write command writes the specified number of lines to the disk. The W command always begins with the first line. The syntax is

```
<x>W
```

where <x> is the number of lines to write to disk. The file will be written to disk using the file name specified when you started EDLIN.

Edit Line. The Edit Line command allows you to edit a line. By simply entering the line number and pressing Enter, EDLIN will display that line and enter the edit mode. You can type a period and press Enter to edit the current line. You can use the editing keys described in Chapter 6 to edit the line.

Creating and Editing a File

Using EDLIN is a simple procedure. The following example shows you how to use EDLIN to create an AUTOEXEC.BAT file. Note that this AUTOEXEC.BAT file is just an example file; more powerful ones are discussed in Chapter 5, "Using DOS."

To start EDLIN and create the file AUTOEXEC.BAT, type the following:

```
EDLIN AUTOEXEC.BAT[Enter]
```

Using EDLIN

If you don't already have an AUTOEXEC.BAT file, EDLIN will respond with the message

```
New file
*
```

Next, type *I* to put EDLIN into the insert mode, since you can only insert new lines into a blank file:

```
*I[Enter]
```

EDLIN will respond with a line number, colon, and the * prompt:

```
1:*PROMPT $P$G[Enter]
2:*DIR[Enter]
3:*[Ctrl-C]
```

Type the first line, press the Enter key; type the second line, press the Enter key; then press Ctrl-C.

To list the file, press the 1 key (to start the listing with line number 1), then press the L key followed by Enter. This will result in the following display:

```
*1L[Enter]
1: PROMPT $P$G
2: DIR
```

This displays the lines you have entered so far. Now let's insert a command, SK, which will load in a program called *SideKick*. To use the insert command, press the 2 key (to insert the new line before line number 2, the DIR command), then press I followed by Enter. As shown in the following display, EDLIN will display line number 2, a colon, and the asterisk prompt. Typing SK and pressing Enter, followed by Ctrl-C, will finish the inserting process.

```
*2I[Enter]
2:*SK[Enter]
3:*[Ctrl-C]
```

CHAPTER 9

Next, list the file to make sure everything is correct. To do so type 1L and press Enter. The system will display the following:

```
*1L[Enter]
1: PROMPT $P$G
2: SK
3:*DIR
```

Once satisfied that the file is correct, type *E* and press Enter as shown:

```
*E[Enter]
```

DOS will save the file and return to the operating system prompt. Modifying a file is done in almost the same manner, except that EDLIN will not respond with the New file message. You would first list the file, then make editing changes as shown above, along with using the commands shown in the first part of this chapter.

Chapter 10

Using DEBUG

Chapter 10

Using DEBUG

DEBUG is a utility program that is most often used by programmers to test programs. DEBUG is a tool geared for the advanced user of DOS, and its use assumes some knowledge of machine language programming. For this reason, some versions of DOS do not include DEBUG. Whether or not you have DEBUG included in your copy of DOS depends on your computer manufacturer's agreement with Microsoft. This program is supplied with the *DOS 3.3 Technical Reference Manual* from IBM.

This discussion of DEBUG is brief. It is only intended to give you an idea of what DEBUG can do, since complete coverage of the subject would be a book in itself. If you intend to use it for program development or debugging, you should refer to your DOS manuals for complete information, or to one of the many books available on assembly language programming.

Be cautious, because DEBUG can damage or even destroy your programs if used incorrectly. DEBUG should only be used with an understanding of the process before you begin, and then *only* on a copy of the program or file, *never* on the original.

In very general terms, DEBUG is a program which takes control of a program you are testing, and it allows you to stop and manipulate the program as you perform testing functions. For example, let's say you have a program that displays the directory in three columns, but the third column always prints in the wrong color. You know that this means that the program is sending a command to the screen to change the screen characters, but which part of the program? Using DEBUG, you can make the program slow down and perform just a few instructions, or even a single one, at a time. When the offending event occurs, you can see what part of the program is causing it and make corrections.

DEBUG Commands

All the actions take place in DEBUG with commands as listed in the following paragraphs. Each of these is just a summary. If you want detailed information, you should refer to the documentation that came with your copy of DOS.

It is important to know that all numbers in the examples are in hexadecimal form. If you don't understand the hexadecimal system, please refer to a programming text.

Briefly, the hexadecimal system uses the ten digits 0–9 and the letters *A–F* to represents the values 0–15. Sixteen is represented by the hexadecimal numeral 10. The letter *A* represents the number 10; *B* is 11; *C* is 12, and so on.

In other words, the number 2A represents $2 \times 16 + 10$, or 42 in decimal. When you have counted up to sixteen 16's (256), you start over with 100 hexadecimal (256). The number 200 in hexadecimal is 512 (or 2×256) in decimal. The next major step is sixteen 256's, represented as 1000 hexadecimal, or 4096 in decimal.

To further complicate things, the addresses in a machine that uses DOS are identified either as simple addresses (like A09F) or as addresses plus offsets. When you see A00:100, it represents the address 2560 (10×256), plus the offset of 256, for a final address of 2816.

Hexadecimal is often called simply *hex*.

A (Assemble). The Assemble command allows you to input program instructions, in assembly language, directly into memory. The syntax is

A address

where *address* is the memory address where the information should be inserted. All address information is input in hexadecimal format.

Using DEBUG

C (Compare). The Compare command compares two areas of the computer's memory. The syntax is

```
C range address
```

The variable *range* is an address range, as an example 100,1FF represents the range of the first of the two areas to be compared. The variable *address* is the beginning address of the second field. For example, the command

```
C 100,1FF 400
```

will compare the areas of address 100 to 1FF with the areas of 400 to 4FF. The first variable, *range,* defines by its own size how far Compare will look through the second range.

D (Dump). The Dump command displays the contents of an area of memory. The syntax is

```
D range
```

where *range* is the area to be displayed. For example, the command

```
D 100,1FF
```

will display the contents of memory from memory location 100 (hex) to 1FF (hex). If no limit is specified, by simply typing *D* and pressing Enter, 256 bytes will be displayed.

E (Enter). The Enter command enters data into the computer's memory. The syntax is

```
E address data
```

The variable *address* is the location in memory where the data is to be loaded. The variable *data* is the information to be loaded at that location. If you do not specify any data, DEBUG will go to the address specified and display the data currently at that address. It will then wait for you to input new data for that address. Once you have entered the data, the address will increment for you to change the data at the next address. To skip an address, press the space bar. To terminate the operation, press the Enter key.

CHAPTER 10

F (Fill). The Fill command fills an area of memory with a specified value. The syntax is

```
F address data
```

The variable *address* is an address range, specified by a starting address and a length, where the variable *data* is to be stored. For example, the command

```
F02AA:100 L 200 00
```

will fill address 02AA:100 through 02AA:2FF with the data 00. The address is given in address:offset format, and all values are in hex. To explain the individual elements of the Fill command, *F* is the command to fill; 02AA:100 represents a hex address (02AA) and a hex offset (100, meaning 256 bytes higher than address 02AA). *L* stands for length, and the number following *L* (200, again in hex) informs DEBUG that the command covers 512 bytes beginning at the address and offset mentioned before. Finally, the 00 represents the information to place in those 512 bytes: the number 0.

G (Go). The Go command tells DEBUG to go to a specified address and execute (run) the program at that address. The syntax is

```
G =address breakpoint(s)
```

The variable =*address* is the location of the program. The equal sign is required to tell DEBUG that this is the location where it should start. The variable *breakpoint* is a location where the program will stop and display the status of the program, showing information such as registers, flags, and so on. There may be more than one variable breakpoint.

H (Hex). The Hex command performs simple hexadecimal arithmetic. The syntax is

```
H value1 value2
```

The variables *value1* and *value2* are hex values. The Hex command responds by displaying two values, first the sum of *value1* and *value2*, and then the difference between *value2* and *value1*.

Using DEBUG

I (Input). The Input command inputs a byte of data from a specified port. The syntax is

I port

The variable *port* is the hex port number from which DE-BUG should get data. For example

I C3F

causes DEBUG to input data from port C3F. DEBUG will then display the value (data) at that port address.

L (Load). The Load command loads a file. The syntax is

L address drive

The variable *address* is an optional address that tells DE-BUG where to load the file. The variable *drive* is optional information telling DEBUG on which drive, and at which location on the drive, the file is located. These are both optional; usually the L command is used by itself following a Name (N) command.

M (Move). The Move command moves a block of data in memory. The syntax is

M range address

The variable *range* is the block of data to be moved, consisting of the starting address and the size of the block. The variable *address* is the destination of the block of data. For example

M AA:120 140 AA:170

will move the 32-byte block from address AA:120 to AA:140, to the area beginning at AA:170. All addresses are in hex notation.

N (Name). The Name command sets up a filename for a subsequent Load or Write command. The syntax is

N filename

The variable *filename* is simply the name of the file to be read in with the Load command, or the name of the file to be written using the Write command.

CHAPTER 10

O (Output). The Output command sends a byte of data to a specified output port. This command complements the Input command. The syntax is

```
O port data
```

The variable *port* represents the hex port number to which DEBUG should output data. The variable *data* is the data that is to be output to the port. For example

```
O C3F 44
```

will output 44 to port C3F.

P (Procedure). The Procedure command executes one instruction of a program under test, and then displays all the registers and flags along with the decoded instruction. The syntax is

```
P =address value
```

The variable *=address* is the location of the program. The equal sign is required to tell DEBUG that this is the location where it should start. The variable *value* is the address where the program will stop and display the status of the program, showing information such as registers, flags, and so on. When more than one Value variable is used, only the registers and flags at the end of the cycle are displayed. If you want to see the results of each command execution, use the Trace command.

Q (Quit). The Quit command does just that, it quits DEBUG. The syntax is

```
Q
```

Note that there are no variables. Using the Quit command terminates DEBUG immediately, it does not save the file in memory being worked on. You are returned immediately to the DOS prompt.

R (Register). The Register command displays the contents of the registers. The syntax is

```
R names
```

The variable *names* specifies which registers are to be displayed. To exit the Register command, press the Enter key.

S (Search). The Search command searches through a specified range of addresses for a list of data. The syntax is

```
S address data
```

The variable *address* consists of a starting address followed by the length of the area to be searched. The variable *data* is the byte or string of data to be searched for. For example

```
S AA:100 1FF 0A
```

will search each byte in the address range AA:100 to AA:1FF for one that contains the value 0A hexadecimal (10 decimal).

T (Trace). The Trace command executes an instruction, then displays the resulting registers and flags. The syntax is

```
T =address number
```

The variable *=address* is the location of the program. The equal sign is required to tell DEBUG that this is the location where it should start. The variable *number* is the number of instructions to be executed before Trace stops and displays the registers, flags, and so on. Trace executes and then displays each instruction. If it isn't necessary to see the results of each instruction, it's better to use the Procedure command.

U (Unassemble). The Unassemble command disassembles a program and displays the program in assembly language format. The syntax is

```
U address
```

The variable *address* gives the starting address of the disassembly, and optionally the range to be disassembled.

For example

U AA:100 L40

will disassemble 64 bytes (40 hex) starting at address AA:100.

W (Write). The Write command writes the file being worked on to disk. The syntax is

W address drive

The optional variable *address* tells DEBUG where in memory to get the file. The optional variable *drive* tells DEBUG on which drive and where on that drive the file is to be located. These are both optional, usually the W command is used by itself following a Name (N) command.

Chapter 11

The AUTOEXEC.BAT File

Chapter 11

The
AUTOEXEC.BAT
File

If you have an AUTOEXEC.BAT file on your computer's hard disk or boot disk (the disk in drive A: when you turn the computer on), it is the first program the computer runs when you turn it on.

It isn't necessary to have an AUTOEXEC.BAT file in your system. If you don't have this file, the computer will simply ask you for the date and time, then take you to the root directory. On systems without a clock/calendar, allowing the computer to prompt you may be preferable. This way you can enter the correct date and time so that the files are tagged accurately. On a system with a clock/calendar card, or on a system with the date and time function built in (as it is on most AT-class computers), you will not need to concern yourself with setting the date and time.

The following line shows a sample of a very basic AUTOEXEC.BAT file. Using it causes the computer to bypass the date and time questions and display the directory.

```
DIR
```

This is easily created by simply typing the lines

```
COPY CON AUTOEXEC.BAT[Enter]
DIR[Ctrl-Z][Enter]
```

CHAPTER 11

The computer will then start up, display the DOS sign-on messages, and then display the contents of the root directory. This version assumes that you are running an AT-class computer, which takes care of the date and time function automatically, or it assumes you are not concerned with the date and time information. An AUTOEXEC.BAT batch file which could be used with computers (usually XT-type) that do not have a date/time card could be created by typing the following:

```
COPY CON AUTOEXEC.BAT[Enter]
DATE[Enter]
TIME[Ctrl-Z][Enter]
```

This version of the AUTOEXEC.BAT file would query you for the date and time information and then take you to the DOS prompt in the root directory.

Most AUTOEXEC.BAT files contain more than the examples above. Since most systems have several directories, the AUTOEXEC.BAT file may start out asking for the date and time, define a search path for DOS, call in some type of memory-resident utility, and then display the directory. An example of this type of AUTOEXEC.BAT file would be:

```
DATE
TIME
PATH=C:\;C:\BATCH;C:\MAIN;C:\KICK;C:\UTILITY
KICK
DIR
```

An AUTOEXEC.BAT file of this size can be created with the COPY CON procedure, but at this point you should consider using an editor such as EDLIN to create your batch files. Another very good editor is part of the *Side-Kick* package from Borland.

Of course, the AUTOEXEC.BAT file can become very complex. For example, the following is a variation of one used with the system on which this book was written:

The AUTOEXEC.BAT File

```
GETTIME
PROMPT $P$G
PATH=C:\;C:\BATCH;C:\MAIN;C:\KICK;C:\UTILITY
RAMDISKH D:
AUTOPARK 6 C
VEGA SAVE:60
KEY \KEY\WP
WF
CD KICK
SK
CD \
SA BRIGHT WHITE ON GREEN
CLS
CD WORDPROC
DIR
```

The above AUTOEXEC.BAT file begins by assuming that a program called GETTIME.COM gets the date and time information from a plug-in calendar card. It next sets up the prompt to show the current drive and defines the path by which DOS searches for the programs you want to run. Next it executes a public domain program called AUTOPARK which causes the hard disk to park its heads after a defined time, and then it informs the user of its actions.

The next command, VEGA, tells the system to shut off the screen after 60 minutes if no keys are pressed on the keyboard. This acts as a "screen saver," preserving the life of the display.

The AUTOEXEC.BAT file then loads a program called *SmartKey*, a program that allows the keyboard keys to be redefined into a different configuration or a single keystroke to represent a string of keystrokes. The AUTOEXEC.BAT file calls an overlay from the KEY directory called *WP*, redefining the keys for the word processing mode. Next the AUTOEXEC.BAT file loads a program called *WF*, a thesaurus (part of the *WordStar* program). Then it loads *SideKick*, followed by a utility from the *Norton Utilities* that sets the screen display background to

green, indicating that the system is now in the word processing mode. The batch file then clears the screen and
goes to the WORDPROC directory, where it displays the
directory. If you are out of breath by now, think how
long doing all this would take you if you had to type the
commands in each time you turned on the system. With
this file, everything takes place automatically, simply by
turning on the computer.

Remember that most items in the AUTOEXEC.BAT
file are simply commands that you might have entered
from the keyboard. Anything in the file that might not
look like a normal DOS command is either the name of a
program or a parameter explained in the documentation
of the software being called.

Chapter 12

DOS Techniques

Chapter 12

DOS Techniques

This chapter covers techniques you can use to make DOS work more effectively for you. In some cases you'll see recommendations for programs in the public domain, meaning they are available for free or for only the cost of copying them. These programs are available from some of the sources listed in Appendix A, "Public Domain and Shareware Software." In addition, you will often see references to the directory organization as shown in Figure 12-1 below.

Figure 12-1. Disk Organization for the Batch File Examples

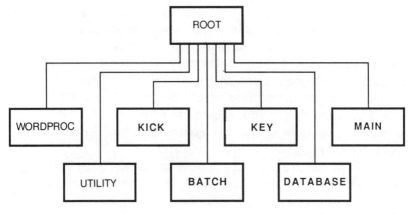

Since your system will probably be organized differently from the system shown in Figure 12-1, just use this figure as a guide. As you will see, changes in the structure of your system are very easy to make.

Making Operation Easier

Usually a person will buy a computer as a simple, powerful tool to accomplish a task (as well as for a source of entertainment and education). With the input of a few characters, you should be able to give the computer complete instructions to carry out a job. Batch files refine the process by allowing you to tell the computer what you want done, and the batch file gives the computer the detailed instructions. Batch files allow you to create a simple name for a complex operation, and, by typing that simple name, the complex operation can be carried out.

If you are a new computer user, you are probably struggling a bit, trying to remember all the things you are supposed to do when you turn the computer on. You may be using a cheat sheet for the commands to move between the directories, files, and programs you want to use. Even if you are comfortable with the process of moving around in the computer directory structure and bringing up new programs, you may still feel that a little simplification in the process would be good. That's what batch files can do for you, regardless of your level of computer experience. After all, computers should make your life simpler, not more complicated.

Computers are general-purpose machines. That is the characteristic that makes them appealing to so many people. Your use for a computer is different from mine, and possibly is different from your co-worker's. Some people need them for databases, some for spreadsheets, some for word processing, some for games, some for programming, some for accounting, and so on. Batch files can help tailor the computer to your needs. They customize the computer to your application, setting it up to perform the tasks you need done. With batch files you can give easily remembered names to the commands you use often.

DOS Techniques

Speeding Up Your System

There are many ways you can speed up the operation of your computer system. Some of them deal with hardware: putting in faster processors, increasing the clock speed, going to faster disk drives, and so on. Other techniques deal with making the system work more easily. Dividing the memory of the computer to create a ramdisk can significantly increase the speed of programs that perform intensive data retrieval from the hard disk. Batch files are then used to move the programs you are running to the ramdisk.

Other ways of speeding up the system include making the system easier to use by replacing a string of commands for complex functions with a single word. For example, a single letter might allow you to display the directory of one of your drives, another letter might display that same directory, but show only the .BAS files (BASIC language program files). Most of the following examples will help you do just that; by substituting a single-word command in place of a string of commands, a batch file can make the operation of the computer much easier and faster.

Using a Ramdisk

One way to speed up your system is to use a *ramdisk*. A ramdisk is a part of the computer's memory that DOS addresses as if it were a disk drive. By copying a program's files to the ramdisk, the computer makes file access faster than access from a mechanical disk drive. The disadvantage of a ramdisk is that when power is turned off, the information is lost. That means you must copy the information in the ramdisk back to a hard or floppy disk before shutting off the power. Another disadvantage of a ramdisk is that it uses some of your system memory to create the simulated disk storage. These trade-offs must be weighed when deciding whether to use a ramdisk. The following are some guidelines to help you make your decision.

CHAPTER 12

Use CHKDSK.COM (Chapter 6, "DOS Commands") to determine how much free memory you have in your system. This is shown as *bytes free* at the bottom of the CHKDSK report. Subtract from that free memory the size of the application program you want to run. Whatever is left over represents the amount of memory you have for your ramdisk. For example, say that CHKDSK gives the following report:

Volume Main Drive created Aug 11, 1988 3:52p

```
21309440  bytes total disk space
   24576  bytes in 5 hidden files
   36864  bytes in 16 directories
12308480  bytes in 379 user files
 8939520  bytes available on disk

  655360  bytes total memory
  364448  bytes free
```

CHKDSK shows that there are 364448 bytes of memory free. Let's assume that you are going to run a very compact spreadsheet program. It shows up on the directory listing as having a file size of 44K. Let's further assume that the data files you are going to analyze are small; there are nine of them totaling 87K. The math is simple (the calculations are rounded off):

Free memory:	364K
Spreadsheet program:	−44K
Data files:	−87K
Amount of RAM left:	233K

Since you'll need some free RAM for the program to run, subtract another 33K (a rough guess); what you have left is 200K. That means you can create a ramdisk of 200K. That would be easily accomplished with the following line inserted into the CONFIG.SYS file:

DEVICE = VDISK.SYS 200 512 64

DOS Techniques

Inserting this line into the CONFIG.SYS file would create a ramdisk with a size of 200K, using 512-byte sectors and allowing 64 directory entries. DOS will automatically assign the next available drive number to the ramdisk.

What has been shown so far is fine if all you are going to do is run the spreadsheet program. But if you need to run a program that needs more memory, you will have to restart the computer with another system disk that contains a different CONFIG.SYS file—one that does not create a ramdisk, or one that creates a ramdisk of a different size. The alternative is to use some form of expanded or extended memory, and locate the ramdisk in that memory area. These memory expansions usually come on boards that plug into your system and extend the system RAM beyond 640K, usually 1,000K to 2,000K (1–2MB). If you are considering using a ramdisk as a permanent feature of your system, you should consider one of these cards.

Now that you have created a ramdisk, and DOS has assigned the drive letter D: to it, what do you do next? Using the above example of a spreadsheet, you use a batch file to move the spreadsheet files to drive D:. Assume that the spreadsheet and the data files are in a directory called MAIN, and the spreadsheet is named CALCLATE.COM. The following is a listing of a typical file that would accomplish the necessary file moving, we'll call it RAMDRIVE.BAT:

```
C:
CD \MAIN
COPY CALCLATE.COM D:
COPY *.DAT D:
D:
DIR
```

The above batch file would start by logging to the C: drive. Then it would log onto the MAIN directory. This assures that, regardless of where you are in the drive and directory structure, you will begin at the right place. The next line copies CALCLATE.COM to the D: drive, and the following line copies all the data files using the file type .DAT. The last two lines log you to the D: drive and display the directory.

Any number of variations on the above file are possible. For example, if you had a large enough ramdisk, you might copy all of your word processing files to it, along with the word processor program, the spelling tester and its dictionaries, and the thesaurus files.

Once you've created the ramdisk and have moved the files to it, you're free to use it just as you would any other drive on the system. There is only one warning you need to remember: When you shut off the system, you will lose all the information—and all the work you've done—if you don't save the files in the ramdisk to either a hard or floppy disk. The following section explains how to save your files.

Shutting Off the System

If you are using part of your system RAM for a ramdisk, you should make sure that you have not left any of your important files in the ramdisk before you turn off your system. Remember, a ramdisk forgets everything when you turn off the power. All your work will be lost unless you copy the files you have changed to either a hard or floppy disk.

What you need to do is create a batch file that saves your new or changed files back to the disk. There are several approaches you might take. One is to remove all the files you don't want to copy back to the disk drive from the ramdisk, then copy the rest. The other is to copy only the files you have possibly changed.

Let's assume that you are using the ramdisk to do word processing, and that you create a batch file called CLEAN.BAT to clean up the ramdisk when you are through. It might contain the following series of commands:

```
C:
CD \WORDPROC
ERASE D:*.COM
ERASE D:*.EXE
ERASE D:*.OVR
COPY D:*.*
DIR D:
```

This first version of a ramdisk saver logs onto the WORDPROC directory on the hard disk, drive C:, from wherever you are (including any other drive or subdirectory); then it erases all the files with a file type of .COM, .EXE, and .OVR on the ramdisk, drive D:. All the remaining files on the ramdisk are then copied to the WORDPROC directory on the hard disk. The files with a file type of .COM, .EXE, and .OVR are erased first to reduce the number of files you must copy. After all, you may have word processing files with a file type of .TXT for text in a book, .DOC for software documentation, .ART for magazine articles, or .LTR for letters to friends. Why waste time copying your word processor and support files (that will probably never change) back to the hard disk?

Sometimes it might not be necessary to copy a large number of different file types back to the disk. For example, in a spreadsheet program, all you may need to do is copy the files with a file type of .DAT back from the ramdisk to the MAIN directory on the hard disk. The following batch file will accomplish this:

```
COPY D:*.DAT C:\MAIN\*.*
```

With the above file, all of the files with a file type of .DAT will be copied from the ramdisk to the directory MAIN on the hard disk. You only need to copy the file type .DAT because it's the only one you want to save. There's no need to erase the program files first.

Remember, you don't have to copy the programs themselves, since they were not removed from the hard or floppy disk when you copied them to the ramdisk, so you don't have to copy them back to the hard disk.

CHAPTER 12

The Directory Display

Let's examine some of the ways you can use batch commands to make the directory easier to understand by making its appearance much cleaner.

Normally, when you use the directory command, you type DIR, and the screen displays something like this (though it usually contains more files):

```
Volume in drive C is HARD DRIVE
Directory of C:\

INCOME  BAS    8723   10-23-87  3:17p
WS      COM   17649   11-11-87  3:45a
2 Files(s) 14285903 bytes free
```

But maybe you'd like to see only the files that end in .BAS, since you are only interested in your BASIC language files. To do this you would type

DIR *.BAS[Enter]

Your display would then look something like this:

```
Volume in drive C is HARD DRIVE
Directory of C:\

INCOME  BAS  8723    10-23-87  3:17p
1 Files(s) 14285903 bytes free
```

However, what you really want to do is type something you can remember easily, for example:

BAS

To create a batch file that will display a directory of all your BASIC files, you need to create a batch file called BAS.BAT that contains the line

DIR *.BAS

The easiest way to do that is by typing

COPY CON BAS.BAT[Enter]
DIR *.BAS[Ctrl-Z][Enter]

The computer should respond with the following message:

130

1 file(s) copied

When you typed the line

COPY CON BAS.BAT

you told the computer to COPY what you typed on the CONsole (keyboard) into a file called BAS.BAT. You then typed

DIR *.BAS[Ctrl-Z][Enter]

and the computer entered this line into a file. The Ctrl-Z told the computer that this would be the end of the file, and, when you pressed Return, the computer saved the file on the disk. This process created a program called BAS.BAT. To run the program, type

BAS[Enter]

When the program runs, the batch file will type the keyboard input for you. In this case, it types the line

DIR *.BAS

as if you had typed it on the keyboard.

If you list the directory, you should now see a new file named BAS.BAT. This is the file you just created. To try it—type BAS. If you have any files in your directory with a file type of .BAS, you should see them listed, no other files. If you don't have any .BAS file types, you should get the following message:

Volume in drive C is HARD DRIVE
Directory of C: \

File not found

You can customize this batch file for your own needs. Let's say you want to be able to list all the memos you wrote simply by typing MEMO. Assume you named them MEMO1 through MEMO97 (or however many you have written). All you need to do is create a batch file called MEMO.BAT with the line in it reading

DIR MEMO*.*

CHAPTER 12

This will list all the files with the name MEMO followed by any other characters. In the same manner as above, type

```
COPY CON MEMO.BAT[Enter]
DIR MEMO*.*[Ctrl-Z][Enter]
```

You will now have a file called MEMO.BAT which, when you type MEMO, will display all files beginning with MEMO.

There are some excellent programs available that allow you to list the directory in ways different from the standard DOS DIR format. Some of them are public domain programs (see Appendix A).

One public domain program is called DD. It displays the directory in two columns instead of one. If you are running out of disk space, and you want to list all of your backup files before deciding whether to erase them, and if you have DD.COM in your DOS directory, you can use a batch file to do this by having it type the following line:

```
DD *.BAK[Enter]
```

This will list all the files with the file type of .BAK. To create this file, type

```
COPY CON BAK.BAT[Enter]
DD *.BAK[Ctrl-Z][Enter]
```

You will now have a file called BAK.BAT which, when you type BAK, will display all files with a file type of .BAK in a two-column format.

After using the batch file BAK.BAT above to list all of the .BAK files, you might decide to erase them. The batch file ERABAK.BAT will do this for you. To create this file, type the following:

```
COPY CON ERABAK.BAT[Enter]
ERASE *.BAK[Ctrl-Z][Enter]
```

This file will erase all of the files with the file type of .BAK in the directory you are logged onto. Note that it will not erase all of the files with a file type of .BAK everywhere on the disk, just those in the directory you are logged onto.

Changing Commands

Sometimes you might prefer to type shorter versions of commands, such as ERA in place of ERASE. Maybe you are coming to DOS from an experience with other operating systems, and you prefer to use some of the same command names for similar functions. In some cases you can simply rename a command. For example, the FOR-MAT command, since it is a file, could be renamed from FORMAT.COM to PREPARE.COM. Some commands, such as DIR or ERASE, are part of the operating system and cannot easily be renamed. (It can be done, using DE-BUG, but that is beyond the scope of this book.) An alternative to renaming a command is to use a batch file to change the name of the command. The batch file would have the name of the command familiar to you, and it could then call the program whose name you want to change.

Some commands require something to operate on. For example, COPY and ERASE require additional information after the command to tell the command what to do with which files. The additional information is called a *parameter*. The parameter is passed through a batch file using a percentage sign followed by a numeral between 0 and 9 (actually you can use more, but let's keep this simple). For example, to create a batch file called ERA.BAT that will erase a file or group of files, type the following:

```
COPY CON ERA.BAT[Enter]
ERASE %1[Ctrl-Z][Enter]
```

Let's assume in this example that you're going to erase all the files named CAT, regardless of their file type. When you use the ERASE command, you might normally type ERASE CAT.*. However, if you prefer to type ERA CAT.*, the batch file ERA.BAT will be executed and the command

ERASE CAT.*

will actually be executed. The batch file has called the ERASE command and the parameter %1, here called CAT.*, will be passed on to the ERASE command. The batch file has substituted CAT.* for the %1 parameter when it executed the ERASE command. This parameter is merely the name of the file, or files, you are going to erase. This same technique can be used with almost any batch file to pass information between a batch file and a program or command.

Making Commands Easier

Sometimes when you are logged onto drive C:, you might find yourself frequently consulting the directories on the A: and B: drives. The following batch files make this job easy. Simply use COPY COM as you did earlier and create A.BAT. Then type in

DIR A:[Ctrl-Z][Enter]

If you have drive B:, follow exactly the same procedure, but substitute the letter *B* as the drive identifier.

When you want to list the directory of drive A:, simply enter *A* followed by Enter. Use a similar procedure to list the directory of drive B:. This reduces six keystrokes to one—DIR A: to A.

Creating Directories Automatically

One of the problems that you may encounter involves copying to a subdirectory. Often you'll find the files are accidentally copied to the root directory. There are two possible reasons for this: Either you forgot to specify the path for the destination or you forgot to change to the new directory before issuing the command to copy the files.

The following batch file eliminates these errors. It assumes you are creating a directory on the C: drive (a hard drive) and are copying all of the files from a disk in the A: drive to the new directory in the hard drive. The first line in the batch file creates the new directory.

Notice the %1 in the first line. This stands for the name of the new directory when you run the batch file. The second line logs you onto the new directory, and the third line copies all the files from the A: drive to the new directory.

With the following lines, create a batch file called NEWDIR.BAT, using the same procedure shown earlier:

```
MD %1
CD %1
COPY A:*.*
```

To run the program, type

```
NEWDIR name
```

where *name* is the name of the new directory you are creating. The name is put into the parameter %1, and the first line creates a directory of the name you type. The second line moves to that directory, and the third line copies all the files from the A: drive to the new directory. Since you are logged onto the new directory, the destination does not have to be specified.

Cleaning Up Your Disks

Hard disk operations are plagued by multiplication of backup files. If you are a prudent user, you will always save a backup each time you update a file. After a period of time, though, you will discover that your directories become clogged with backups, to the extent that you might be hard-pressed to say which one is the most current, or which ones are from the current piece of work and which ones are left over from the last project.

When this happens, back up your files on a floppy disk and then eliminate all the backup files. This can be done by typing

`ERASE *.BAK[Enter]`

Use a command like this carefully. It is very easy to make a simple typo, such as .bat instead of .bak, which would erase useful files you never intended to erase.

An easier way to clean the backup files out of a directory is to use a batch file like the following. Remember to give it a memorable name. To create this batch file, type the following:

`COPY CON ERABAK.BAT[Enter]`
`ERASE *.BAK[Ctrl-Z][Enter]`

This will create a batch file named ERABAK.BAT which will allow you to erase all the backup files, and clean up your directory, simply by typing ERABAK and pressing Enter. Once this batch file is working properly, it prevents accidents. However, this file will only erase the backup files in the directory you are logged onto. The following example will erase all the backup files in all the directories shown (beginning with the directory you are currently logged onto, then the WORDPROC directory, the PROGRAM directory, and the ARCHIVE directory):

```
ERASE *.BAK
CD \WORDPROC
ERASE *.BAK
CD \PROGRAM
ERASE *.BAK
CD \ARCHIVE
ERASE *.BAK
CD \
```

Backing Up Your System

Backing up your files is one of the most important tasks you will do with your computer. No disk is permanent, nor immune to trouble. A cup of coffee spilled on a floppy disk or rough handling of the hard disk can prove that. Even magnetic fields from motors, or magnetized screwdrivers, can ruin a disk. Both old age and extensive use can also take their toll. The result is all the same: lost files.

There are several programs that take care of backing up your system. For example, DOS provides a set of programs, BACKUP and RESTORE, that will back up a system, and do a good job. The problem with BACKUP and RESTORE is that when you restore a damaged disk, it must have the same directory structure as the original. This presents a problem if your hard disk has failed and you are trying to restore the files to a new drive and may not have the directory structured the same. In addition, BACKUP and RESTORE use a special compression process that allows you to get more information on a disk, but at the loss of being able to simply put the disk into any computer and copy a file.

There are alternatives to BACKUP and RESTORE. Though slower, you can use the COPY command. It will copy all the files you name from one drive to another, and the copies can be easily read by any standard DOS computer. Creating a batch file to do this can take on many forms. The following shows just a few possibilities. The first is CLONE.BAT, which consists simply of

COPY *.* A:

This batch file will copy all of the files in the directory you are logged onto to the A: drive. This might be useful for backing up all the batch files in the BATCH directory. Just log onto the BATCH directory, put a blank disk in the A: drive, type CLONE, and press Enter. All the files will be copied to drive A:.

The next file, BACKTEXT.BAT, is a little more complicated:

C:
CD \WORDPROC
COPY *.TXT A:

The above batch file will go to the WORDPROC directory on the C: drive and backup all of the .TXT text files to the disk in the A: drive. To use this file, you can be logged into any location on any drive. And, assuming your PATH command can get you to this batch file, you put a blank disk in the A: drive, type BACKTEXT and press Enter. All the files will be copied to drive A:.

There is one problem that both of the above batch files have: They copy *all* the files to the backup disk. This might include files that you haven't worked on for months, and for which you already have several backup copies. To address this problem, use a new DOS 3.3 command, XCOPY.

XCOPY allows you to specify a date, and only those files with a date AFTER the one specified will be copied to the destination drive. The following batch file, BACKDATE.BAT, is an example of this.

```
C:
CD \WORDPROC
XCOPY *.* A: /D:MM-DD-YY
```

The above batch file will go to the C: drive, through the root directory to the WORDPROC directory, and backup all of the .TXT text files, with file dates after the date specified by MM-DD-YY, to the disk in the A: drive. Note: Substitute the date you want to use as a cutoff for the MM-DD-YY as shown in the above example.

With the above batch file, you'll have to modify the date each time you use the batch file. Although this may be handy sometimes, there is an alternative to having to make this change each time. The following batch file, BACKFROM.BAT, allows you to specify the date on the command line.

```
C:
CD \WORDPROC
XCOPY *.* A: /D:%1
```

This batch file uses a parameter, %1, to specify the date. When you use this version, type the command line as follows, substituting the date you want to use as a cut-off date:

BACKFROM 12-25-88

The above command line will take all files modified after December 25, 1988, and copy them to the A: drive. Note that this will only copy the files from the directory you are logged into when you type the BACKFROM command.

The following version of a backup batch file, BACKALL.BAT, is the most complete. It will go through all the directories shown, backing up all of the files after the date specified. It can be expanded simply by adding variations of the last two lines for each of the file types or directories you need to cover.

```
C:
CD \WORDPROC
XCOPY *.TXT A: /D:%1
XCOPY *.DOC A: /D:%1
XCOPY *. A: /D:%1
CD \DATABASE
XCOPY *.DAT A: /D:%1
CD \MAIN
XCOPY *.* A: /D:%1
```

The above batch file begins by going to the C: drive through the root directory to the WORDPROC directory, and it backs up all of the .TXT text files with file dates after the date specified by MM-DD-YY, putting the backups on the disk in the A: drive. It then backs up all of the .DOC files, and then all of the files with no file type specified. It then changes to the DATABASE directory and backs up all the data files with a file type of .DAT; then it changes to the MAIN directory and backs up all the files with a date after that specified.

Other Handy Utilities

There are a large number of additional things batch files can do, as you may have guessed by now. Batch files can, with a single command, perform long and complex operations. Since this is a book for the newcomer to DOS 3.3, and to DOS in general, I won't be presenting any really complex batch files. However, a batch file could easily, upon being started, initiate programs that call in and retrieve the daily stock quotations, add the results to a spreadsheet, and, if a critical value on any stocks is reached, place buy or sell orders. This is not fantasy, it is being done today. However, you have to start with easier programs (batch files are programs). Why not start with the following utility, START.BAT?

When my system first comes on, the AUTOEXEC.BAT file sets up the prompt, defines the path, and sets the screen to red. When I see a red screen, the system is ready to run the programs I chose. If I am doing word processing, I need programs such as *SmartKey* and *Side-Kick*. I use a batch file called START.BAT to load them in. The following is a listing of this batch file:

```
KEY \KEY\WP
WF
CD KICK
SK
CD \
SA BRIGHT WHITE ON GREEN
CLS
```

By typing START and pressing Enter, the START.BAT file executes the *SmartKey* program, which loads a list of key definitions (WP—Word Processing) stored in the KEY directory. START.BAT then executes the WF program, a thesaurus program that is used with *WordStar*. Next, it changes directories to the KICK directory and executes the *SideKick* (SK) program. START.BAT then changes back to the root directory with the CD \ command. (This directory change is necessary since *Side-Kick* looks for the help file in the directory you are logged onto when you execute the program, not the directory where it finds *SideKick*.) Next, START.BAT uses one of the *Norton Utilities* to set the screen to white letters on a green screen. When I see a green screen, the system is set to the word processing mode. The last instruction, CLS, clears the screen. You can see how my computer accommodates itself to my preferences. You can also see how easily these preferences can be changed or added to.

Sometimes, when buried in some subdirectory of a disk, you may want a simple way to get back to the root directory of the C: drive. This batch file, C.BAT will get you there. Just type C and press Enter, and you'll find yourself back at the root directory, on the C: drive, with a display of the directory. This is done as follows:

```
C:
CD \
CLS
DIR
```

The first line changes you from whatever drive you may be logged onto to the C: drive. The second line takes you back to the root directory. The third line clears the screen, and the fourth line displays the root directory.

Changing Screen Colors to Show System Status

Norton Utilities have been mentioned before in this and other chapters. The utilities make up a set of powerful and useful programs. One of the *Norton Utilities* is a program called SA.COM. *SA* stands for Screen Attributes. One of the things it can do is change the color of your screen (assuming you have a color system). When my system starts up, the last command in the AUTOEXEC.BAT file is SA. The full command line is

```
SA BRIGHT WHITE ON RED
```

This sets my screen to a full red screen with white lettering, indicating at a glance that the system has booted up and is ready for use. If I am going to work with the word processor, I type WP and the batch file initializes the system for word processing, changing the screen to green to tell me that the word processor is ready. If I am going to use the database, I type DATA

CHAPTER 12

and the batch file initializes the system for database
work, changing the screen to blue to tell me that it is
ready to run the database program. Typical listings of
these batch files are shown below. The following
AUTOEXEC.BAT file defines the prompt characteristics,
defines the path, and sets the screen to red.

```
PROMPT $P$G
PATH=C:\;C:\BATCH;C:\MAIN;C:\DOS33;C:\PUBLIC
SA BRIGHT WHITE ON RED
```

The following file, WORDPROC.BAT, changes to the
WORDPROC directory, changes the screen to green, and
displays the directory.

```
C:
CD \WORDPROC
SA BRIGHT WHITE ON GREEN
DIR
```

The following batch file, DATABASE.BAT, changes
to the DATABASE directory, changes the screen to blue,
and displays the directory.

```
C:
CD \DATABASE
SA BRIGHT WHITE ON BLUE
DIR
```

Changing the Prompt to Show System Status

If you don't want to (or can't) change the background
color to show changes in the system status, there is another way to display the system status. You can use the
PROMPT command.

The PROMPT command allows you to customize the
prompt. The prompt is the character displayed by the
computer to let you know it's ready to receive a command. This prompt can also display a message. For example, the following prompt tells you that there are no
utilities installed, how to install the utilities, and how to
start up the DOS shell (the DOS shell is discussed in
Chapter 13, "A DOS Shell").

PROMPT The system has no utilities installed. $_Type
START to install the utilities. $_Type SHELL to use the
shell.$_$G

The above command string must be entered as a single line, since the character entered by the computer
when you press the Enter key will disrupt proper operation of this command.

Obviously you don't want to type a line this long
each time you change the prompt, so the prompt should
be made into a batch file. In this case, it might be called
PROMPT1.BAT and be put into the end of the AUTO-
EXEC.BAT file. This would have the effect of informing
you of the status of the system (no utilities installed), and
telling you how to install the utilities and how to go to
the shell.

Something else you might want is to display the date
and time each time you exit a program. Since the prompt
is redisplayed each time you exit a program, it could be
changed to accomplish the display date and time function. The following example shows one way you could
accomplish this:

```
PROMPT
$_$_$_$_$_$_$_$_$_$_$_$_$_$_$_$_$_$_$_$_$_$
_$D$_$T$_$P$_$G
```

Again, the command string must be entered as a single line, since the character entered by the computer
when you press the Enter key will disrupt proper operation of this command.

Note that there are 21 of the dollar sign–underscore
($_) character sets in a row. Each of these tells the com-
puter to move the cursor down one row. This has the effect of clearing the screen without using the clear screen
(CLS) command before the PROMPT command. Though
this technique is slower than using CLS, it shows what
can be done with the PROMPT command.

After the 21 $_ character sets, the $D character set
tells the computer to display the date, another $_ moves
the cursor to the beginning of the next row, and the $T

character set tells the computer to display the time. After another $_ to move the cursor to the next row, the $P tells the computer to display which directory you are logged onto. The final $_ and $G display a system prompt, where you type the next command. This entire sequence, from the 21 $_ character sets to the $G character set, has the effect of clearing the screen, displaying the current date, time, and logged directory every time you press the Enter key or exit a program.

Moving Between Directories

Using the CD or CD \ command to move between directories is not always convenient. It might be easier if you could simply type the directory name and have the computer do all the work. A word of caution: You must make sure that you don't have any directory names that are the same as program names, otherwise you could end up running a program every time you tried to change to that directory. For example, having a batch file called WORDPROC which would automatically take you to the WORDPROC directory would be fine, as long as your *WordStar* program is identified as such, and is not called WORDPROC. Here is the batch file WORDPROC that changes to the WORDPROC directory:

```
C:
CD \WORDPROC
```

The first line of this batch file would log you onto the C: drive. The second line would take you to the WORDPROC directory.

Chapter 13
A DOS Shell

Chapter 13

A DOS Shell

It's often easier to run DOS from a menu, especially if you are new to DOS, or if you simply prefer to have the computer remember the commands required for you to get into, and run, your applications programs. This is often done with a shell program. However, another way to do the job is with batch files. Since they are so easy to create, this chapter will show you how to create a DOS shell, using batch files, that allows you to run DOS from a menu.

This version has a difference, however. Although it appears that you are running the program from a menu, since you have a menu on the screen and you pick your application by typing a number and pressing Enter, you are actually running it from DOS.

The Shell Menu

The illusion of a shell is created by having a batch file use the ECHO command to put a menu on the screen. The menu will show a number of functions, each with a corresponding number. When you press the number, then Enter, the computer will look for a program named with that number. What the computer will find is a series of batch files named with numbers. DOS will then execute the corresponding batch file, and you will have the illusion of a shell. You can modify the functions as your requirements change, and of course each of the files in this chapter will have full details on how the file works and instructions on how to change it.

CHAPTER 13

Let's start by looking at a sample menu that the batch file might display (Figure 13-1).

Figure 13-1. Sample Menu

```
***************************************************************************
*                                                                         *
*                           Computer Menu                                 *
*                                                                         *
***************************************************************************

:                                                                         :
:     To do any of the following, press the corresponding number,        :
:     then press the [Enter] key                                          :
:                                                                         :
:        1    Word processing                                             :
:        2    Database                                                    :
:        3    Spreadsheet                                                 :
:        4    Games                                                       :
:        5    Display the directory                                       :
:        6    Backup word processor text files (.TXT) to drive B          :
:        7    Check the hard drive                                        :
:                                                                         :
:                                                                         :
:                                                                         :
:                                                                         :
:  To run any other program, simply type the program name and            :
:  press [Enter] - Remember, you're still in DOS!                         :
:.........................................................................:
```

A DOS Shell

It starts with a sign-on banner and then lists the functions you can perform. This menu assumes that you are logged onto a hard disk and that your directory looks like the directory shown in Figure 13-2. In addition, it assumes that the AUTOEXEC.BAT file, or some other program, has set up the PATH command to read, as a minimum:

PATH = C:\;C:\SHELL

Figure 13-2. Disk Organization for the Shell Example

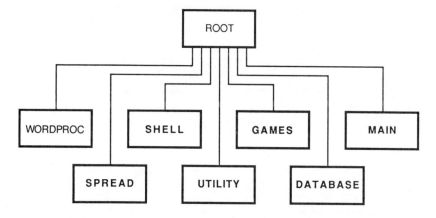

Your system is almost certainly organized differently from the system shown in Figure 13-1. You will have to make corresponding changes in the menu. This is easily done, because the menu is just text displayed on the screen by a batch file. Figure 13-3 shows the listing of this initial batch file, called SHELL.BAT.

Figure 13-3. SHELL.BAT

```
C:
CD\
CD SHELL
ECHO OFF
CLS
ECHO **********************************************************************************
ECHO *                                                                                *
ECHO *                            Computer Menu                                       *
ECHO *                                                                                *
ECHO **********************************************************************************
ECHO :                                                                                :
ECHO :     To do any of the following, press the corresponding number,                :
ECHO :     then press the [Enter] key                                                 :
ECHO :                                                                                :
ECHO :         1   Word processing                                                    :
ECHO :         2   Database                                                           :
ECHO :         3   Spreadsheet                                                        :
ECHO :         4   Games                                                              :
ECHO :         5   Display the directory                                             :
ECHO :         6   Back up word processor text files (.TXT) to drive B               :
ECHO :         7   Check the hard drive                                               :
ECHO :                                                                                :
ECHO :                                                                                :
ECHO :                                                                                :
ECHO :                                                                                :
ECHO : To run any other program, simply type the program name and                     :
ECHO : press [Enter] - Remember, you're still in DOS!                                 :
ECHO :................................................................................:
```

The Batch Files

The above SHELL.BAT file creates the screen display;
then, after displaying the text, it goes to a DOS prompt.
When you press a corresponding number, followed by
the Enter key, you are actually running a batch file, in
this example, files named 1.BAT through 7.BAT. These
contain the commands as shown below. Let's begin with
1.BAT. This file takes you directly into the *WordStar* word
processing program.

```
C:
CD \WORDPROC
WS
CD \SHELL
SHELL
```

This file begins by logging onto the C: drive, and
then it changes to the WORDPROC directory in the root
directory. It does this because you might be invoking the
command from anywhere on the system, and the command needs a known starting point. If you don't have a
C: drive, change this to A:, B:, or whatever drive you consider to be your root directory.

The file then executes the command WS. This in-
vokes the program *WordStar*. At this point you can do
your word processing with *WordStar*, and when you are
ready to leave, you exit *WordStar* in the normal manner
(typing the letter X from the file menu).

When you exit *WordStar*, control is turned back over to
the batch file, which will then log you onto the SHELL directory and run the SHELL.BAT program. The SHELL.BAT
menu will be displayed on the screen.

If there is a file you edit frequently, such as a letter
you are working on but can't quite finish or a book, you
can change the computer menu to have one of the numbers say something like

```
8 Edit the letter to the boss
```

That will call a batch file similar to the above, but with one difference. The line WS (the fourth line in the listing above) could be changed to read

```
WS LTR2BOSS
```

This would start *WordStar* and go directly into the file LTR2BOSS. Just as above, when you exit the letter and *WordStar*, control will return to the batch file, which will continue the processing cycle.

The next batch file, 2.BAT takes you to the DATABASE directory; then it displays the directory. In this manner you can determine if the database file you want to run is present or if you copied it to another disk.

```
C:
CD \DATABASE
DIR
```

This file, like 1.BAT, starts out by going to the DATABASE directory in the root directory of drive C:.

This approach is useful in many other applications. For example, if you want to use it to access a utility, you could make an entry in the SHELL.BAT file that takes you to a utility directory. The computer would then display a listing of all the files in that directory, and you could select the utility. In this case the listing for 2.BAT might read

```
C:
CD \UTILITY
DIR *.COM
```

This logs you to the UTILITY directory and displays a listing of all the files with a file type of .COM. You might also want the files with a file type of .EXE or .BAT, so the last line might change to

```
DIR *.COM
DIR *.EXE
DIR *.BAT
```

A DOS Shell

There is also the wide directory display option that you might use, so the listings would then read

```
DIR *.COM /W
DIR *.EXE /W
DIR *.BAT /W
```

which allows you to display almost five times the number of files, since the /W option displays the files five across.

The next batch file, 3.BAT operates in the same manner as 1.BAT. It starts by logging onto the SPREAD directory and executing *SuperCalc3*. When you exit *SuperCalc3*, control is turned back over to the batch file, which will then change to the SHELL directory and will run the SHELL.BAT program. This will result in you being logged onto the SHELL directory and the SHELL.BAT menu being displayed on the screen.

```
C:
CD \SPREAD
SC3
CD \SHELL
SHELL
```

The next example, 4.BAT, is a bit frivolous. It shows how you can have one (or more) selections display a message instead of performing a function. You could, for example, have this file be a message you create, reminding you of daily tasks to be done, a file you select once a day as a memory jog.

```
ECHO OFF
CLS
ECHO Sorry, you can't play games today.
ECHO You have WORK to do!
PAUSE
SHELL
```

The following batch file, 5.BAT, displays the contents of the currently logged directory and drive, in this case

153

the directory of the SHELL directory.

```
CLS
DIR
PAUSE
SHELL
```

If you want it to display the contents of, for example, the text files (files to which you have given the file type of .TXT) in the WORDPROC directory, the contents of 5.BAT would read as follows:

```
CLS
DIR \WORDPROC\*.TXT
PAUSE
SHELL
```

This would display all the .TXT files in the WORDPROC directory. It could be modified in the same manner to cover any files in any directory.

The following file, 6.BAT copies all files with the file type of .TXT from the directory WORDPROC on the C: drive to a disk on the A: drive. This would be used to back up all of the text files in the WORDPROC directory of the hard drive (drive C:).

```
C:
CD \WORDPROC
COPY *.TXT B:
DIR B:
PAUSE
CD \SHELL
SHELL
```

This batch file, 7.BAT, runs the program CHKDSK to determine the number of files on the disk and the available empty space.

```
ECHO OFF
CLS
CHKDSK
PAUSE
SHELL
```

Chapter 14

Branching Within a Batch File

Chapter 14

Branching Within a Batch File

DOS batch files are capable of far more than just simple substitution for a series of keystrokes. You can use them to write programs. This chapter presents a batch file that tests for the existence of a file on a disk and then copies the file only if it is not already on the disk. This can be especially handy if the files are large, taking a long time to copy. In another instance, you might not want to copy a file to a disk if there is already a file on that disk by the same name, even if it is not the same file (this happens often with text files).

Using Flowcharts

Before you start on some of the more complex batch files, you should learn at least the fundamentals of using flowcharts. Large batch files, like all kinds of programs, can become very complex, and errors are easily made. If you develop the habit of drawing flowcharts early, you will have far fewer problems later on developing large batch files. In fact, complex batch files will become easy once you develop good skills at constructing flowcharts.

Drawing a flowchart consists of making a map of the route a program will take as it runs. Figure 14-1 shows some of the simple blocks that are used in flowcharts. These three symbols will handle virtually everything you will do with batch files.

CHAPTER 14

Figure 14-1. Flowchart Symbols

This symbol is normally used as a label showing where some task is to start or end.

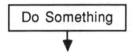

This symbol is normally used to show where a task is to be performed.

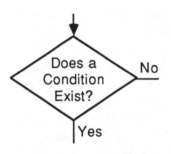

This symbol is normally used to show where a decision is made and the program jumps to different locations depending on the result of the test.

The Batch File

For this book, I have created an example of the symbols and use of flowcharts for batch files. The example assumes you are copying two batch files to floppy disks. However, you don't want to copy the batch files to the floppy if they already exist there with the same name, but you do want to copy the files if the disk doesn't contain files of the same name. To see how this is done, look at Figure 14-2 and compare it with the listing of the batch file which follows.

Branching Within a Batch File

Figure 14-2. A Simple Flowchart

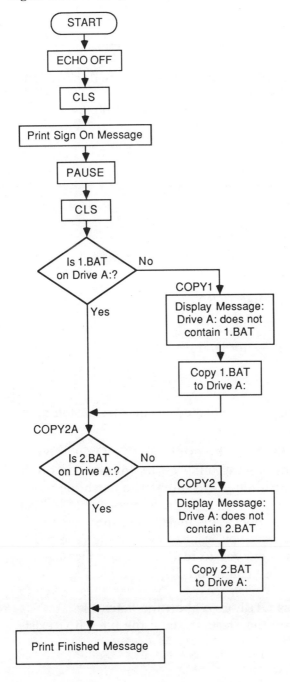

CHAPTER 14

Program 14-1. File Copy Program

```
ECHO OFF
CLS
ECHO                     File Copy Program.
ECHO
ECHO This program checks for files on the destination
_disk, then copies
ECHO only the files that are necessary to make a
_complete set.
ECHO
PAUSE
CLS
IF NOT EXIST A:1.BAT GOTO COPY1
GOTO COPY2A
:COPY1
ECHO Drive A: does not contain 1.BAT.
ECHO
COPY C:1.BAT A:
:COPY2A
IF NOT EXIST A:2.BAT GOTO COPY2
GOTO QUIT
:COPY2
ECHO Drive A: does not contain 2.BAT.
COPY C:2.BAT A:
:QUIT
ECHO
ECHO All of the files are copied to the destination disk
_in Drive A:
```

The batch file starts by using the ECHO OFF command to prevent printing unnecessary information on the screen as the batch file is executing. The batch file then clears the screen and prints a sign-on message to tell you what the program does. This makes sure that you are running the program you want to be running. The program pauses to allow you to read the screen message, and since the pause command displays a message telling you to *Strike a key when ready . . .,* you can press a key to proceed or press CTRL-C to abort the batch file.

The program then tests to see if the file 1.BAT exists

on drive A:. If it does not exist, the program goes to a label (a word on a line by itself, preceded by a colon) called :COPY1. The next line causes the computer to print a message that the file does not exist on drive A:, and then the program copies the file from drive C: to drive A:. If the program does exist on drive A:, the program goes to the next line: GOTO COPY2A, which jumps to the label :COPY2A. Whether or not the file existed or was copied, the program ends up at :COPY2A.

A very similar sequence is then performed on a file called 2.BAT. In this case, if the file does not exist, the program jumps to :COPY2, and if the file does exist the program jumps to the label :QUIT. The program then prints the message that the files are copied to the destination disk in drive A:.

There are several lines in the listing that contain the command ECHO with no characters following it. What is actually there is a nonprinting character that allows the ECHO command to print a blank line. Otherwise the ECHO command will print nothing, and the program title and text lines will be crowded together. To include a blank line in your batch file:

• Type the word ECHO followed by a space.
• Press and hold the Alt key.
• Type 255 using the number keys on the right side of the keyboard. Don't use the numbers across the top of the keyboard.
• Release the Alt key.
• Press the Return key.

This example shows the relationship between the flowchart and the batch file listing. By using these techniques, you can develop batch files for backing up directories selectively, sending files over networks, or almost any other function you can perform using command lines or collections of command lines.

One technique to consider before actually running a large batch file is to step through it one step at a time.

CHAPTER 14

The easy way to do this is to simply type each of the command lines as it appears in the batch file and see that the program will do what you intended. Another way is to insert a PAUSE command between each of the commands in the batch file. In this way the batch file will pause between each task and tell you to press a key to continue. If the program starts to do something wrong, you can abort the process by typing CTRL-C.

Appendices

Appendix A

Public Domain and Shareware Software

Public domain software is free. Programs in the public domain range from extensive word processing and database programs to utilities and games. At a level between the free public domain software and expensive commercial packages are shareware (or freeware) programs that are user-supported. Under the shareware concept, the software is made available through most public domain distribution outlets, but the author of the program depends on the user to send in a small payment after the user decides the program is useful. The prices range from only a few dollars to $20.00, with a few of the very powerful programs slightly more expensive. Both public domain and user-supported software offer some very exotic and useful programs.

Software Sources

The list of free or shareware software includes thousands of titles. Among them, you will find extremely powerful databases, spreadsheets, word processors, disk utilities, games, languages, music, graphics, and business, to name only a few types of programs. The list goes on and on. In writing this book, I came across more than 10,000 shareware programs. Rather than list them here, it would be more useful to list some of the hundreds of sources of public domain software.

APPENDIX A

Bulletin boards are springing up all over the country, and they are loaded with free software. Some bulletin boards have illegal copies of commercial software, which you should avoid at all costs: At least one manufacturer has vowed to strike back against copyright infringements with a "Trojan horse" program that would destroy the mass storage unit of anyone downloading copyrighted programs. Most computer clubs are a good source of legitimate software, and computer-oriented tabloid newspapers will usually list some sources in the back pages. Computer swap-meets, organized by computer clubs and even ham radio clubs, are excellent sources of software. In case none of these sources are handy, try some of the sources listed below. You can write or call them for their catalogs, which are usually free or available for a nominal fee of a dollar or two. The price of the disks, which usually contain more than one program, is generally between $3.00 and $6.00.

Future Systems
Box 3040
Vista, CA 92083
(619) 941-3244 (orders and information, 24 hours)
(619) 941-9761 (office, 10–6)

Generic Computer Systems
22612 Foothill Blvd.
Suite 200C
Hayward, CA 94541
(415) 581-1494

MicroCom Systems
3673 Enochs St.
Santa Clara, CA 95051
(408) 737-9000

Shareware Express
31877 Del Obispo
Suite 102W
San Juan Capistrano, CA 92675

Public Domain and Shareware Software

SoftWareHouse
3080 Olcott Dr.
Suite #125A
Santa Clara, CA 95054
(408) 748-0461 (voice)
(408) 748-0232 (bulletin board)

The SoftWareHouse also provides full technical advice and support for software and hardware, both by voice and over their bulletin board. The best time to call for support is in the evenings, since most of their staff is busy during the days in other jobs. You can call the bulletin board, and, after becoming a member for a nominal charge (about $10.00), you can download all the software you want. Of course, it's also good manners to provide, in return, public domain software you have written yourself or collected from other sources.

And of course, you should also look at the disk-and-magazine combinations available from commercial presses, such as *COMPUTE!'s PC Magazine*. With a subscription to these magazines, you not only receive a magazine dedicated to users of IBM PCs and compatibles, but with every issue you get a disk full of software. The software includes applications for home and business, utilities, educational programs for kids, games, graphics demos, and more.

Appendix B

DOS 3.3 Files

The following list shows all the files distributed by IBM
with their version of DOS 3.3. The columns Name, Type,
Size, Date, and Time reflect the same information you
would receive using the DIR command. You can use the
following information to verify that you have the complete set of files. The Disk column shows which disk the
file is on for the 5¼-inch disks. A 3½-inch disk contains
all the files on a single disk.

Name	Type	Size	Date	Time	Disk
4201	CPI	17089	3-18-87	12:00p	Startup
5202	CPI	459	3-17-87	12:00p	Startup
ANSI	SYS	1678	3-17-87	12:00p	Startup
APPEND	EXE	5825	3-17-87	12:00p	Operating
ASSIGN	COM	1561	3-17-87	12:00p	Operating
ATTRIB	EXE	9529	3-17-87	12:00p	Operating
BACKUP	COM	31913	3-18-87	12:00p	Operating
BASIC	COM	1063	3-17-87	12:00p	Operating
BASIC	PIF	369	3-17-87	12:00p	Operating
BASICA	COM	36403	3-17-87	12:00p	Operating
BASICA	PIF	369	3-17-87	12:00p	Operating
CHKDSK	COM	9850	3-18-87	12:00p	Operating
COMMAND	COM	25307	3-17-87	12:00p	Operating
COMMAND	COM	25307	3-17-87	12:00p	Startup
COMP	COM	4214	3-17-87	12:00p	Operating
COUNTRY	SYS	11285	3-17-87	12:00p	Startup
DEBUG	COM	15897	3-17-87	12:00p	Operating
DISKCOMP	COM	5879	3-17-87	12:00p	Operating
DISKCOPY	COM	6295	3-17-87	12:00p	Operating
DISPLAY	SYS	11290	3-17-87	12:00p	Startup
DRIVER	SYS	1196	3-17-87	12:00p	Startup
EDLIN	COM	7526	3-17-87	12:00p	Operating

APPENDIX B

Name	Type	Size	Date	Time	Disk
EGA	CPI	49065	3-18-87	12:00p	Startup
FASTOPEN	EXE	3919	3-17-87	12:00p	Startup
FDISK	COM	48216	3-18-87	12:00p	Startup
FIND	EXE	6434	3-17-87	12:00p	Operating
FORMAT	COM	11616	3-18-87	12:00p	Operating
FORMAT	COM	11616	3-18-87	12:00p	Startup
GRAFTABL	COM	6128	3-17-87	12:00p	Operating
GRAPHICS	COM	3300	3-17-87	12:00p	Operating
JOIN	EXE	8969	3-17-87	12:00p	Operating
KEYB	COM	9056	3-17-87	12:00p	Startup
KEYBOARD	SYS	19766	3-17-87	12:00p	Startup
LABEL	COM	2377	3-17-87	12:00p	Operating
LCD	CPI	10752	3-17-87	12:00p	Startup
MODE	COM	15487	3-17-87	12:00p	Startup
MORE	COM	313	3-17-87	12:00p	Operating
MORTGAGE	BAS	6251	3-17-87	12:00p	Operating
NLSFUNC	EXE	3060	3-17-87	12:00p	Startup
PRINT	COM	9026	3-17-87	12:00p	Operating
PRINTER	SYS	13590	3-17-87	12:00p	Startup
RECOVER	COM	4299	3-18-87	12:00p	Operating
REPLACE	EXE	11775	3-17-87	12:00p	Operating
REPLACE	EXE	11775	3-17-87	12:00p	Startup
RESTORE	COM	34643	3-17-87	12:00p	Operating
SELECT	COM	4163	3-17-87	12:00p	Startup
SHARE	EXE	8608	3-17-87	12:00p	Operating
SORT	EXE	1977	3-17-87	12:00p	Operating
SUBST	EXE	9909	3-17-87	12:00p	Operating
SYS	COM	4766	3-17-87	12:00p	Startup
TREE	COM	3571	3-17-87	12:00p	Operating
VDISK	SYS	3455	3-17-87	12:00p	Startup
XCOPY	EXE	11247	3-17-87	12:00p	Operating
XCOPY	EXE	11247	3-17-87	12:00p	Startup

Appendix C

DOS Commands

Not all commands are available with all versions of DOS. Check your manual to determine if a command is provided with your version.

Intrinsic Commands
BREAK
CHCP
CHDIR
CLS
COPY
CTTY
DATE
DEL
DIR
ERASE
MKDIR
PATH
PROMPT
RENAME
RMDIR
SET
TIME
TYPE
VER
VERIFY
VOL

Transient Commands

APPEND
ASSIGN
ATTRIB
BACKUP
BASIC and BASICA
CHKDSK
COMP
DEBUG
DISKCOMP
DISKCOPY
EDLIN
EXE2BIN
FASTOPEN
FDISK
FIND
FORMAT
GRAFTABL
GRAPHICS
JOIN
KEYB
LABEL
MODE
MORE
NLSFUNC
PRINT
PROMPT
RECOVER
REPLACE
RESTORE
SELECT
SHARE
SORT
SUBST
SYS
TREE
XCOPY

Frequently Used Commands
CHDIR or CD
COPY
DATE
DEL or ERASE
DIR
MKDIR or MD
MORE
RMDIR or RD,
TIME
TYPE

Occasionally Used Commands
BACKUP and RESTORE
CHKDSK
CLS
PATH
FORMAT
MODE
RECOVER
REN or RENAME

Seldom Used Commands
APPEND
ASSIGN
ATTRIB
BREAK
CHCP
COMMAND
COMP
CTTY
DISKCOMP
DISKCOPY
EXE2BIN
FASTOPEN
FDISK
FIND
GRAPHICS

APPENDIX C

Seldom Used Commands

GRAFTABL
JOIN
KEYB
LABEL
NLSFUNC
PROMPT
REPLACE
SELECT
SET
SHARE
SORT
SUBST
SYS
TREE
VER
VERIFY
VOL
XCOPY

Commands

Where examples are not given, refer to your manual.

APPEND	Provides a function similar to the PATH command, in that it allows DOS to locate files outside the current directory. (PATH is limited to file types .COM, .EXE, and .BAT; APPEND can locate files of any extension type.)	Seldom used	Transient

APPEND \TEXT[Enter]

ASSIGN	Tells DOS to route disk instructions to a different drive than the one specified.	Seldom used	Transient

ASSIGN A=B[Enter]

ATTRIB	Sets the attributes for files.	Seldom used	Transient

ATTRIB +R GAME.COM

DOS Commands

BACKUP and RESTORE commands	BACKUP copies the files from your hard disk to floppy disks in a special compacted format. RE-STORE can then restore the proper operation of the hard disk in the event of a failure.	Occasionally used	Transient

```
BACKUP source destination[Enter]
RESTORE source destination[Enter]
```

BREAK	Allows you to tell DOS when to check for a Ctrl-Break condition, sometimes used where you may want to break into the operation of the program.	Seldom used	Intrinsic

```
BREAK ON[Enter]
```

CHDIR or CD	Used to change from one directory to another. You can use either CD or CHDIR, the commands are identical.	Frequently used	Intrinsic

```
CD MAIN[Enter]
```

CHCP	Selects the code page that DOS uses for changing screen display characters (normally used in countries outside the U.S.).	Seldom used	Intrinsic
CHKDSK	Allows you to determine the integrity of a disk and tells you how much space is being used on the disk and how much is free.	Occasionally used	Transient

```
CHKDSK[Enter]
```

CLS	Clears the screen.	Occasionally used	Intrinsic

```
CLS[Enter]
```

COMP	Compares the contents of two files.	Seldom used	Transient

```
COMP File1 File2[Enter]
```

COPY	Used every time you copy files from one disk to another or make copies of files in different directories.	Frequently used	Intrinsic

```
COPY source destination[Enter]
```

CTTY	Changes the standard console (keyboard and display) to another device.	Seldom used	Intrinsic

```
CTTY COM1[Enter]
```

DATE	Used to set the date in the computer.	Frequently used	Intrinsic
DATE[Enter]			
DEL or ERASE	Identical commands that remove a file or group of files from the disk.	Frequently used	Intrinsic
DEL fn.ft[Enter]			
DIR	Allows you to see what's on your disk. It will show all the files.	Frequently used	Intrinsic
DIR[Enter]			
DISKCOMP	Compares the contents of two disks. (It will not work on a hard disk.)	Seldom used	Transient
DISKCOMP disk1 disk2[Enter]			
DISKCOPY	Makes an identical copy of a disk.	Seldom used	Transient
DISKCOPY source destination[Enter]			
EXE2BIN	Converts EXE files to COM or BIN files (no longer included with 3.3).	Seldom used	Transient
EXE2BIN GAME.EXE[Enter]			
FASTOPEN	Allows you to access files in your directories faster by storing the location of the disk files in the computer's memory.	Seldom used	Transient
FDISK	Used only once—to set up a hard disk.	Seldom used	Transient
FIND	Used to print all lines in a file or group of files that contain a specified string of characters.	Seldom used	Transient
FIND "TRUFFLES" FILE.TXT[Enter]			
FORMAT	Allows you to format a disk, removing all the previous information from the disk to prepare it for fresh data.	Occasionally used	Transient
FORMAT A:[Enter]			
GRAFTABL	Loads a table of additional character data into memory for color or graphics mode.	Seldom used	Transient
GRAPHICS	Allows the screen display to be printed.	Seldom used	External
JOIN	Allows you to join two directories, on two separate drives, to form a single directory.	Seldom used	Transient

176

DOS Commands

KEYB	Loads a program that allows you to use non-English keyboards.	Seldom used	Transient
LABEL	Allows you to add, delete, or change the volume label on a disk.	Seldom used	Transient
MKDIR or MD	Creates a new directory. The two commands function identically.	Frequently used	Intrinsic

MD TEST[Enter]

MODE	Sets up the video adapter (such as a monochrome, CGA, or EGA system); sets up the parameters of the serial port (COM1:, for example); redirects printer assignments from the default printer port (LPT1:) to any of the other possible ports, allowing the computer to talk to more than one printer.	Occasionally used	Transient

MODE BW80[Enter]
MODE COM1:1200,N,8,1

MORE	A pipeline command that allows you to read a screen of text before it scrolls off the screen.	Frequently used	Transient

TYPE CAT.TXT I MORE[Enter]

NLSFUNC	A new command for DOS 3.3; supports additional screen display characters along with the CHCP command.	Seldom used	Transient
PATH	Allows you to set the path through the directory structure where DOS will search for a program.	Occasionally used	Intrinsic

PATH = \ DOS

PROMPT	Allows you to change the system prompt.	Seldom used	Transient

PROMPT PG[Enter]

RECOVER	Used in conjunction with the BACKUP command; see BACKUP.		
REN or RENAME	Changes the name of a specified file. REN and RENAME function identically.	Occasionally used	Intrinsic

REN AUTOEXEC.BAT AUTOBACK.BAT[Enter]

REPLACE	Allows you to replace files on one disk with files from another disk REPLACE is an enhanced version of the COPY command.	Seldom used	Transient

RMDIR or RD Removes an empty directory; the Frequently used Intrinsic
two function identically.

RD TEST[Enter]

SELECT Installs DOS on a new disk and Seldom used Transient
allows you to define the country
code and keyboard layout.

SELECT 001 US[Enter]

SHARE Provides file-sharing support for Seldom used Transient
systems with more than one
user.

SORT A filter that takes data from a Seldom used Transient
file, sorts it, and outputs the data
to another file.

SUBST Allows you to substitute a drive Seldom used Transient
letter for a path.

SUBST D: C:\WORDPROC\ARCHIVE[Enter]

SYS Copies the two hidden DOS files Seldom used Transient
onto a disk.

TIME Just like the DATE command,
except it deals with the time
stored in the system instead of
the date.

TIME[Enter]

TREE Lists the directories on the disk. Seldom used Transient

TREE[Enter]

TYPE Allows you to display the con- Frequently used Intrinsic
tents of a text or ASCII file, such
as one you create with a word
processor.

TYPE HOME.TXT[Enter]

VER Tells you which version of the Seldom used Intrinsic
operating system is being used.

VER[Enter]

VERIFY Causes DOS to verify the integ- Seldom used Intrinsic
rity of data after writing it to a
disk.

VERIFY ON[Enter]

VOL Displays the volume label on a Seldom used Intrinsic
disk.

VOL[Enter]

XCOPY Allows you to copy a file or Seldom used Transient
group of files selectively.

Appendix D

DOS Editing Keys

F1 This key repeats one keystroke from the previously typed command line.

F2 This key copies all the characters in the buffer onto the command line, until it reaches a specified key. For example, if you typed the command line

```
DIR B:*.COM
```

to look at all the files with an extension of .COM, and now you want to look at all the files with an extension of .EXE, you could type

```
[F2]**.EXE[Enter]
```

The computer would copy all the characters in the buffer up to the asterisk (DIR B:*) into the command line. You would then type *.EXE[Enter] and the command line would be sent to the computer as

```
DIR B:*.EXE
```

F3 This key copies all the characters in the buffer onto the command line. For example, if you want to look at the directory on drive C:, you would type

```
DIR C:[Enter]
```

The computer will then display the directory of drive C:. If you forgot to look for a file and want to display the directory again, instead of typing the command line DIR C: and pressing Enter again, you could simply type

```
[F3][Enter]
```

F4 This key deletes all the characters in the buffer until it reaches a specified key. For example, if you type the command line

```
DIR B:TEST.*
```

to look at all the files with a filename of TEST.*, and now you want to erase all of them, you could type

```
DEL [F4]B[F3][Enter]
```

After you've typed DEL, pressing F4 followed by the letter *B* deletes all characters in the buffer up to the *B*. Pressing F3 enters all the remaining characters into the command line.

F5 This key copies the contents of the command line, as it appears on the screen, to the buffer. The old contents of the buffer are lost.

Del key Pressing this key deletes characters in the command line at the location of the cursor. The left cursor key also performs this function.

Esc key This key cancels the current command line. For example, if you get to the end of the command line and realize that you are doing the wrong thing (such as looking at the directory when you should be changing directories), pressing the Esc key will take you back to your starting point.

Ins key Pressing this key turns on insert mode. Normally, when you type a character, the character types over the characters already in the buffer. Insert mode allows you to insert characters into the buffer without destroying the characters already there.

Ctrl-Alt-+ Pressing the Ctrl, Alt, and + keys at the same time turns up the volume of the keyboard click. Hold the keys down until the keyboard click is at the volume level you want.

Ctrl-Alt-− Pressing the Ctrl, Alt, and − keys at the same time turns down the volume of the keyboard click.

DOS Editing Keys

F6 Pressing this key has the same action as Ctrl-Z: It enters a character known as the *end of file marker*. If you are entering a list of commands from the keyboard to be used by the computer as a batch file, the F6 or Ctrl-Z would be the last character entered.

F7 Pressing this key results in the same action as Ctrl-@. It causes a NUL character to be entered into the command line.

Ctrl-Break This key combination cancels operation of a program in progress. Since the program in progress could be writing to a disk drive, which, if instantly abandoned, could result in destruction of data, this combination should be considered an emergency procedure only.

Ctrl-Num Lock This combination temporarily halts operation of a program in progress. This is handy for stopping information, such as a directory listing, that is scrolling off the screen too fast. Pressing any key causes the operation of the program you were running to resume where it left off.

Shift-PrtSc This key combination prints the contents of the screen to the printer. When this is happening, the remaining operations, such as the execution of any programs, are halted. Note that this usually works only with text information, not graphics. If you need to print graphics information, consult your DOS manuals to see if you have special provisions for this, or check with your computer dealer.

Ctrl-PrtSc This key combination prints the characters displayed on the screen to the printer at the same time as they are displayed on the screen. This does not dump the entire screen to the printer, only the characters that are displayed after the Ctrl-PrtSc keys are pressed.

Tab key This key moves the cursor to the next tab position. The tabs in DOS are normally set every eighth column.

Appendix E

Error Messages

This appendix lists the error messages you are likely to encounter while using DOS, along with the cause for the error message and the cure for the problem. Error messages found in DOS are listed first, followed by error messages found in some of the commands and programs of DOS. The error messages are listed in alphabetical order, and only the most common ones are shown. A complete listing would take over 100 pages.

Error messages are displayed when DOS encounters an error, needs to inform you of some system status, or needs to prompt you for an action. The DOS messages listed in this appendix are applicable to DOS version 3.3.

Disk and Device Errors

If a disk or device error occurs at any time during a command or application program, DOS displays an error message in the following format:

<type><action> drive <x:> Abort, Retry, Ignore, Fail?

Note that the Ignore option is not displayed in conjunction with floppy disk errors. In the above message, <type> is one of the following error conditions:

Bad call format error
Bad command error
Bad unit error
Data error
FCB unavailable
General failure
Invalid disk change

Lock violation
Non-DOS disk error
No paper error
Not ready error
Read fault error
Sector not found error
Seek error
Sharing violation
Write fault error
Write-protect error

The *<action>* is either *reading* or *writing*.

The word *drive <x:>* indicates the drive on which the error occurred. For example, if you attempt to write to the disk in drive A: and the disk has a write-protect tab on it, the following error message is displayed:

```
Write protect error writing drive A
Abort, Retry, Fail?
```

DOS waits for you to respond in one of the following ways:

A (Abort)	This will stop the program which is requesting the disk read or write.
R (Retry)	This will repeat the operation. Use this response if you corrected the error (for instance, if you removed the write-protect tab in the above example).
F (Fail) or I (Ignore)	This tells DOS to ignore the error condition and proceed with the program.

Error Messages from DOS

Message: Abort, Retry, Fail, Ignore?
Cause: This message is normally displayed when the computer cannot find a disk in the drive you tell it to go to.
Cure: Make sure you have a disk in the drive. If not, put one in, and type *R* for retry. If there is a disk in the drive, the data on the disk may be bad. You can either type *I* for ignore, and hope to recover some of the data;

F for fail; or *A* for abort. You will then need to find the cause of the error. Remember: If data is worth keeping, its probably worth having a backup copy, too.

Message: Are you sure (Y/N)?
Cause: This message is displayed when you tell DOS to delete all the files in a directory, or when you are trying to format a hard disk. Take your time when you see this message, and make sure you want to do what you've told the computer to do.
Cure: Press *Y* if you want to delete files or to format the hard disk. Answering N will take you safely back to DOS.

Message: Bad command or filename
Cause: This message is displayed when DOS can't find the program or file you told it to find.
Cure: Verify the spelling of the file, and make sure that it is on the disk where you told DOS to find it. This would be either the currently logged disk and directory, or another disk or subdirectory if you prefixed the name with an alternative location.

Message: Bad or missing (filename)
Cause: This message is displayed when DOS cannot find a specified device driver, usually specified by the CONFIG.SYS file, or if the device driver has an error.
Cure: Make sure that the device driver is located in the root directory of the boot disk. If it is, it may be bad, in which case you may need to copy a good version from your backup disk.

Message: Bad or missing Command Interpreter
Cause: This message is displayed when DOS cannot find the file COMMAND.COM.
Cure: Make sure COMMAND.COM is located in the root directory of the boot disk. Note: You may have substituted another command processor as specified in the CONFIG.SYS file. If so, make sure the filename of the substitute command processor matches that shown in the CONFIG.SYS file.

Message: BREAK is off (or on)

Cause: This message is displayed to tell you the status of the Ctrl-Break and Ctrl-C checking. No response is required.

Message: Divide overflow

Cause: This message is displayed by DOS if a program causes a software malfunction.

Cure: If you created the program that caused this error message, you must use a debugger or other programming tool to find the problem and fix it. If you purchased the program, you should try running the program from the backup or master disks, since the program is causing the problem. If this fails to correct the problem, contact the dealer where you bought the program, since this indicates an error in the program.

Message: Error in .EXE file

Cause: This message indicates that the program you are attempting to run has an invalid internal format.

Cure: If you created the program that caused this error message, you must relink the program or make a new copy. If you purchased the program, you should try running the program from the backup or master disks, since the program is causing the problem. If this fails to correct the problem, contact the dealer where you bought the program, since this indicates an error in the program.

Message: Error writing to device

Cause: This message is displayed if too much data is being sent to a device, usually a serial or parallel port.

Cure: Check to see that the program has all the proper provisions for handshaking. This is usually handled through protocols such as XON/XOFF, ETX/ACK, DSR/DTR, or other similar provisions. Refer to the manual that came with your software to determine the solution to your problem.

Message: EXEC failure

Cause: This message is displayed when an error is found while reading a command, or the Files line in the CONFIG.SYS file is set too low.

Cure: Verify that the program is good by using another copy from a backup disk, or increase the number that follows *FILES* = in the CONFIG.SYS file.

Message: File allocation table bad

Cause: This message is displayed when a disk is defective.

Cure: Run the program CHKDSK to verify that the disk is bad. If it is, try to recover the data by copying what you can to another disk. You will have to copy the files which cannot be recovered from the bad disk from your backup disks instead.

Message: File cannot be copied onto itself

Cause: This message is displayed when you try to copy a file onto itself, usually by not specifying different sources and destinations for the file.

Cure: Make sure you are specifying the correct source and destination for the file or files you are copying.

Message: File creation error

Cause: This message is displayed when you try to add a new file or replace a file that already exists, and the file has the read-only attribute set. These files cannot be replaced.

Cure: Make sure you want to overwrite the existing file on the destination disk, then change the attribute of the file to read-write. This is normally done with a utility such as the *Norton Utilities*.

Message: Incorrect DOS version
Cause: This message is displayed when you are trying to run some of the new utilities on a computer running an older version of DOS.
Cure: Make sure the version of DOS in the machine is the latest version (use the VER command) or use an older version of the utility.

Message: Insert diskette for drive <x:> and strike any key when ready
Cause: This message informs you of what you need to do next when copying or formatting.
Cure: Insert a disk into the drive as instructed.

Message: Insert diskette with batch file and press any key when ready
Cause: This message is displayed when DOS does not find the batch file you specified in the drive. This is normally only displayed after the computer has begun executing the batch file, and it needs the rest of the information in the batch file.
Cure: Insert the disk with the batch file into the drive and press any key, normally the Enter key.

Message: Insufficient disk space
Cause: This message is displayed when the disk is full.
Cure: Delete any unnecessary files from the disk. In some cases you may be able to simply swap disks for another one, either blank or at least with more room.

Message: Intermediate file error during pipe
Cause: This message is displayed when the piping process finds an error in one of the temporary files.
Cure: Check the integrity of the disk with CHKDSK, or try again with a new disk.

Message: Internal stack failure
Cause: This message is displayed when the stack space has been used up, usually due to a large number of interrupts being processed by the computer.

Error Messages

Cure: Increase the size of the stack by using the STACK command in the CONFIG.SYS.

Message: Invalid COMMAND.COM. Insert COMMAND.COM disk in default drive and strike any key when ready
Cause: This message is displayed when COMMAND.COM must be loaded again from the disk, but the file cannot be found.
Cure: Insert a disk containing COMMAND.COM into the default drive.

Message: Invalid date
Cause: This message is displayed when you enter an invalid date in response to the date prompt.
Cure: Re-enter the date correctly.

Message: Invalid device
Cause: This message is displayed when the device specified is not CON, NUL, AUX, or PRN.
Cure: Specify the proper device.

Message: Invalid drive in search path
Cause: This message is displayed when an invalid drive is specified in the PATH string.
Cure: Revise the PATH command to include only valid paths.

Message: Invalid path or filename
Cause: This message is displayed when an invalid path or filename is specified for the COPY command.
Cure: Verify the path name and filename and correct it as necessary.

Message: Invalid time
Cause: This message is displayed when you specify an invalid time when responding to the TIME prompt when DOS is starting up.
Cure: Enter a valid time in the 24-hour format. Note that only the hours and minutes need to be entered.

Message: Invalid working directory

Cause: This message is displayed when the directory on the disk is bad.

Cure: Although some utility programs can recover some of the problems caused by a bad directory, normally you will have to replace the disk, using the files from your backup copy.

Message: Label not found

Cause: This message is displayed when a GOTO command in a batch file points to a nonexistent label.

Cure: Revise the batch file to correct the problem.

Message: Memory allocation error

Cause: This message is displayed when a program writes into the wrong area of the computer's memory. This error is usually fatal.

Cure: Restart the computer. If the error occurs again, make a new copy of DOS on the system disk from your master disk, and also use another copy of the program you are running. If these procedures don't cure the problem, contact the dealer from whom you purchased the software.

Message: Must specify ON or OFF

Cause: This message is displayed when the command requires an ON or OFF argument in the command line.

Cure: Re-enter the command with the proper argument.

Message: No free file handles. Cannot start COMMAND, exiting

Cause: DOS cannot open a file because the Files command in the CONFIG.SYS file is not large enough.

Cure: Edit the CONFIG.SYS file to increase the size of the Files line. This is normally FILES = 20 for a hard disk system.

Message: No path

Cause: This information message is displayed when you type the PATH command with no parameters, and there is no current search path. No action is required unless you want to create a path for the search.

Message: Out of environment space
Cause: This message is displayed when there is not enough room in the program environment to accept more data.
Cure: Remove unnecessary strings from the environment, then re-enter the command.

Message: Program too big to fit in memory
Cause: This message is displayed when the program requires more memory than is available.
Cure: If you have any memory resident programs, you may have to delete some or all of them. If you do not have a full complement of memory, usually 640K in most machines, you may also have to add more memory.

Message: Sector size too large in file (filename)
Cause: This message is displayed when the device driver loaded by the CONFIG.SYS file uses a sector size larger than that allowed.
Cure: Reduce the sector size to conform to the sector size of DOS.

Message: Specified MS-DOS search directory bad
Cause: This message is displayed when the SHELL command in the CONFIG.SYS file is incorrect. Usually the place you told DOS to find COMMAND.COM does not exist, or COMMAND.COM is not in the place you told DOS to look.
Cure: Make sure that the SHELL command is started from the root directory or that the SHELL command points to the location of COMMAND.COM.

Message: Strike a key when ready...
Cause: This prompt is always displayed with another message, or after using a PAUSE command in a batch file. The other messages displayed with this one will tell you what to do.

Message: Terminate batch job (Y/N)?
Cause: This message is displayed if you press a Ctrl-C while running a batch file.
Cure: Press Y to terminate the batch file or N to continue. You can use either upper- or lowercase letters.

Message: Unable to create a directory
Cause: This message is displayed when DOS cannot create the directory you specified.
Cure: Verify that there is not a directory, or a file, already on the disk with the specified name. If there is, either change the name of the directory you are trying to create or change the name of the file that conflicts. This message is also displayed if the disk is full, in which case you will have to either erase some files or use another disk.

Message: Unrecognized command in CONFIG.SYS
Cause: This message is displayed when there is a bad command in the CONFIG.SYS file.
Cure: Delete or change the name of the command in the CONFIG.SYS file.

Error Messages from Commands (Programs)

The following error messages are issued by commands or programs, such as EDLIN or MODE, that are on the DOS disk. The error messages are listed grouped by the associated command, with those occurring in infrequently used programs, or in multiple commands or programs, listed at the end of this appendix.

CHKDSK

Message: All specified files are contiguous
Associated Command: CHKDSK
Cause: This is an informational message. It indicates that all files are allocated contiguously on the disk and there is no fragmentation.
Cure: No action required.

Error Messages

Message: Allocation error in file, size adjusted
Associated Command: CHKDSK
Cause: This message is displayed when the size of the file indicated in the directory is not consistent with the amount of data actually allocated to the file. The name of the file in error precedes this message.
Cure: If the /F option was specified for CHKDSK, the file is truncated at the end of the last valid cluster.

If the /F option was not specified, this is an informational message only, and no corrective action has been taken by CHKDSK. CHKDSK must be rerun with the /F option specified to correct the error.

Message: Cannot CHDIR to <path> - tree past this point not processed
Associated Command: CHKDSK
Cause: This message is displayed if it is unable to reach the specified subdirectory. All subdirectories beneath this directory are not verified.
Cure: No action required.

Message: Cannot CHDIR to root.
Processing cannot continue
Associated Command: CHKDSK
Cause: This message is displayed if it is unable to return to the root directory while it is verifying the tree directory structure. CHKDSK is unable to continue checking the subdirectories in the root.
Cure: No action required.

Message: Cannot CHKDSK a Network drive
Associated Command: CHKDSK
Cause: This message is displayed if a drive is specified that is redirected over a network. CHKDSK can only operate on local disk drives.
Cure: Do not specify a disk drive that is not local.

Message: Cannot recover . entry, processing continued
Associated Command: CHKDSK

Cause: This error message is displayed when the active directory (indicated by the single period) is defective.
Cure: No action required.

Message: Cannot recover .. entry
Associated Command: CHKDSK
Cause: This error message is displayed when the parent directory (indicated by the two periods) is defective.
Cure: No action required.

Message: Convert lost chains to files (Y/N)?
Associated Command: CHKDSK
Cause: This error message is displayed when it detects lost clusters or chains (multiple clusters).
Cure: If you answer Y, each chain is converted to a file with the filename FILE*n*.CHK, where *n* is a four-digit sequential number starting with 0000. If you answer N, CHKDSK frees the lost chains, and their space can be reallocated by DOS. These actions only occur if the /F option is specified. If not, CHKDSK asks the question, but no action is taken, regardless of the answer.

Message: Corrections will not be written to disk
Associated Command: CHKDSK
Cause: This error message is displayed when an error is detected on the disk and the /F option isn't specified.
Cure: Run CHKDSK again with the /F option specified.

Message: Directory is joined
Associated Command: CHKDSK
Cause: This error message is displayed if a directory on the disk being checked is joined.
Cure: Unjoin the directory and run CHKDSK again.

Message: Directory is totally empty, no . or ..
Associated Command: CHKDSK
Cause: This error message is displayed if a subdirectory does not contain the parent or current directory entries.
Cure: Delete the subdirectory with RMDIR and recreate it using MKDIR.

Error Messages

Message: Disk error reading FAT <x:>
Associated Command: CHKDSK
Cause: This error message is displayed when one of the two File Allocation Tables (FATs) for drive X: has a defective sector in it. DOS automatically uses the good FAT.
Cure: Copy the files to another disk and reformat the disk. If the sectors for the FAT are still defective, discard the disk.

Message: Disk error writing FAT <x:>
Associated Command: CHKDSK
Cause: This error message is displayed when one of the two File Allocation Tables (FATs) for drive X: has a defective sector in it. DOS automatically uses the good FAT.
Cure: Copy the files to another disk and reformat the disk. If the sectors for the FAT are still defective, discard the disk.

Message: [.][..] Does not exist
Associated Command: CHKDSK
Cause: This error message is displayed if either the . or .. entry in a subdirectory is invalid.

Message: Entry has a bad (attribute or link or size)
Associated Command: CHKDSK
Cause: This error message is displayed when an error condition is detected in one of the subdirectory entries. The message is preceded by one or two periods to indicate which entry.
Cure: None. CHKDSK attempts to correct the error if the /F option is specified.

Message: Errors found, F parameter not specified
          Corrections will not be written to disk
Associated Command: CHKDSK
Cause: This error message is displayed when it detects an error and the /F option is not specified.
Cure: Rerun CHKDSK with the /F option specified in order to correct the errors.

Message: <fn.ft> contains noncontiguous blocks
Associated Command: CHKDSK
Cause: This error message is displayed when the file specified is not allocated contiguously on the disk.
Cure: If you specify the /F switch, CHKDSK fixes this error.

Message: <fn.ft> is cross linked on cluster
Associated Command: CHKDSK
Cause: This error message is displayed when two or more files are cross-linked.
Cure: Make a copy of the file you want to keep, and then delete the files that are cross-linked.

Message: First cluster number is invalid, entry truncated
Associated Command: CHKDSK
Cause: This error message is displayed if the file directory entry contains an invalid pointer to the data area. If you specified the /F option, the file is truncated to a zero length file.
Cure: No action required.

Message: Insufficient room in root directory.
Erase files in root and repeat CHKDSK
Associated Command: CHKDSK
Cause: This error message is displayed if your root directory is full.
Cure: Delete some files in your root directory to make room for the lost files.

Message: Invalid subdirectory entry
Associated Command: CHKDSK
Cause: This error message is displayed when the subdirectory specified either does not exist or is invalid.
Cure: Make sure you typed the subdirectory name correctly.

Message: Probable non-DOS disk.
Continue (Y/N)?
Associated Command: CHKDSK

Cause: This error message is displayed when the disk you are using is not recognized by this version of DOS. Either the disk was created by another system with a format that is not supported on this version of DOS or it is not a DOS disk.

Cure: If the /F option was used, reenter the command without it. The possible corrections are displayed. Then, RECOVER the disk with the /F option or reformat it.

Message: Processing cannot continue
Associated Command: CHKDSK
Cause: This error message is displayed when there is not enough memory in your system to process CHKDSK for this disk.
Cure: Remove some drivers or ramdisks, or obtain more memory for your system.

Message: Unrecoverable error in Directory - Convert directory to file (Y/N)?
Associated Command: CHKDSK
Cause: This error message is displayed when there is an unrecoverable error in a directory.
Cure: If you respond Y to this prompt, CHKDSK converts the bad directory into a file. You can then fix the directory yourself or delete it.

COMP

Message: EOF mark not found
Associated Command: COMP
Cause: This informational message is displayed when one or both of the files being compared do not contain end-of-file markers.
Cure: No action required.

Message: Files are different sizes
Associated Command: COMP
Cause: This informational message is displayed when the two files are different sizes. The compare operation is terminated.
Cure: No action required.

Message: 10 Mismatches - ending compare
Associated Command: COMP
Cause: This informational message is displayed when ten mismatches are found. The compare operation is terminated.

COPY

Message: Cannot do binary reads from a device
Associated Command: COPY
Cause: This message is displayed when an attempt is made to copy a file from a device and the /B option is specified. This mode is invalid due to the fact that COPY needs to be able to detect the end-of-file marker from the device.
Cure: Reenter the command and omit the /B option or specify the /A option after the device name on the command line.

Message: Content of destination lost before copy
Associated Command: COPY
Cause: This error message is displayed when the same file is specified as both the source and target drive. For example:

COPY FILE1+FILE2 FILE1

FILE1 is overwritten before it can be copied.
Cure: Copy to a temporary file, delete the duplicate file, and rename the temporary file to the desired filename.

DISKCOMP

Message: Compare error on
          side xx, track yy
Associated Command: DISKCOMP
Cause: There are one or more locations on the indicated side and track of the two disks that contain differing information.
Cure: No action required.

Error Messages

Message: Diskette/Drive not compatible
Associated Command: DISKCOMP
Cause: The disks being compared are of differing densities.
Cure: Only compare disks of similar densities.

Message: Diskettes compare ok
Associated Command: DISKCOMP
Cause: This informational message indicates the two disks contain identical information.
Cure: No action required.

Message: Invalid parameter.
Do not specify filename(s).
Command Format: DISKCOMP d: d: [/1][/8]
Associated Command: DISKCOMP
Cause: This error message is displayed when one or more filenames are specified or invalid parameters are given. DISKCOMP only accepts drive designators.
Cure: Reenter the command with the correct parameters.

Message: SOURCE diskette bad or incompatible
Associated Command: DISKCOMP
Cause: One of the disks is unformatted or incompatible with the drive.
Cure: Use a properly formatted disk.

DISKCOPY

Message: Copy Another (Y/N)?
Associated Command: DISKCOPY
Cause: This message is displayed after it completes copying a disk.
Cure: Press Y if you want to copy another disk, N if you don't.

Message: Copy complete
Associated Command: DISKCOPY
Cause: This is an informational message displayed after it completes copying a disk.
Cure: No action required.

Message: Copy not completed
Associated Command: DISKCOPY
Cause: This error message is displayed when it can't copy the entire disk. This error may be due to a defect on either the source or target disk.
Cure: If the error is on the target disk, use a new disk which has no defects. If the error is on the source disk, use COPY to copy the files to another disk.

Message: Copying...
Associated Command: DISKCOPY
Cause: This informational message is displayed to indicate that it is copying a disk.
Cure: No action required.

Message: Disks must be the same size.
Associated Command: DISKCOPY
Cause: This error message is displayed if you attempt to use DISKCOPY with two disks with different formats and capacities.
Cure: Use disks with the same format or use the COPY command to transfer files and SYS to transfer the system files (if desired).

Message: Drive types or diskette types not compatible
Associated Command: DISKCOPY
Cause: This error message is displayed when you try to copy disks of differing densities.
Cure: Only copy disks of similar densities.

Message: Formatting While Copying
Associated Command: DISKCOPY
Cause: This informational message is displayed when the target disk is not recognized as a formatted disk.
DISKCOPY formats it as it copies from the source disk.
Cure: No action required.

Message: Insert target diskette into drive <x:>
Associated Command: DISKCOPY

Cause: This error message is displayed if you are running DISKCOPY and your source and target drives are the same.

Cure: Reinsert the target disk into the specified drive.

Message: Invalid drive specification.
    Specified drive does not exist,
    or is nonremovable.

Associated Command: DISKCOPY

Cause: This error message is displayed when a drive designator is specified for a drive that doesn't exist or is nonremovable.

Cure: Reenter the command with a drive that exists and is removable.

Message: Invalid parameter.
    Do not specify filename(s).
    Command Format: DISKCOPY d: d: [/1]

Associated Command: DISKCOPY

Cause: This error message is displayed when one or more filenames are specified. DISKCOPY only accepts drive designators.

Cure: Reenter the command with the correct parameters.

Message: Source and target diskettes are not the same format

Associated Command: DISKCOPY

Cause: This error message is displayed when the disk types differ. For example, you cannot copy from a single-sided disk to a double-sided disk.

Cure: Reformat the target disk so that it is the same type as the source disk.

Message: Target disk is write-protected

Associated Command: DISKCOPY

Cause: This error message is displayed when the target disk has a write-protect tab covering the write-enable notch.

Cure: Remove the tab and reinsert the disk.

Message: Target Diskette may be unusable
Associated Command: DISKCOPY
Cause: This error message is displayed because of read, write, or verify errors in the copying process. The target disk may be incomplete.
Cure: Compare the two disks with DISKCOMP. Try again. A new target disk may be necessary.

Message: Unrecoverable Write Error on Drive <x:> Side <x>, Track <x>
Associated Command: DISKCOPY
Cause: This error message is displayed after several unsuccessful attempts are made to write data to the specified track and sector on the disk in the indicated drive.
Cure: The disk is bad. Recover as many files as possible, copy the files to another disk, and try reformatting.

EDLIN

Message: Abort Edit (Y/N)?
Associated Command: EDLIN
Cause: This message is displayed when you use the Q (Quit) command.
Cure: Enter Y if you want to exit without saving the changes, N if you want to cancel the command and continue editing. Use the E command to exit EDLIN and save editing changes.

Message: Cannot edit .BAK file—rename file
Associated Command: EDLIN
Cause: This error message is displayed when the file you are trying to edit has an extension of .BAK.
Cure: Rename the file with a different extension, or copy the file to a new file with an extension other than .BAK.

Message: Disk full. Edits lost
Associated Command: EDLIN

Cause: This error message is displayed when it is unable to save your file due to a lack of disk space.

Cure: Delete enough files to make room for your document and reenter it with EDLIN.

Message: Disk full—write not completed
Associated Command: EDLIN
Cause: This error message is displayed when it is unable to save your file due to a lack of disk space.

Cure: Delete enough files to make room for your document and reenter it with EDLIN.

Message: End of input file
Associated Command: EDLIN
Cause: This informational message is displayed when the entire file has been read into memory. If the file has been read in sections (using the Append command) this message is displayed when the last section is read.

Cure: No action required.

Message: Entry error
Associated Command: EDLIN
Cause: This error message is displayed when it detects a syntax error in a command.

Cure: Retype the command with the correct syntax.

Message: File is READ-ONLY
Associated Command: EDLIN
Cause: This error message is displayed if you try to change a file that is designated as read-only.

Cure: Use the ATTRIB command to change the file's attributes.

Message: Filenames must be specified
Associated Command: EDLIN
Cause: This error message is displayed if you don't specify a file at the time you start EDLIN.

Cure: Specify a file to edit on the command line to start EDLIN.

APPENDIX E

Message: Line too long
Associated Command: EDLIN
Cause: This error message is displayed during a replace command. The string given as the replacement causes the line to exceed 253 characters in length.
Cure: Divide the long line into two lines and retry the REPLACE command.

Message: New file
Associated Command: EDLIN
Cause: This message is displayed if EDLIN can't find an existing file with the name you specified.
Cure: If you want to create a new file, ignore this message. If you don't want to create a new file, make sure you correctly type the name of the file you want to edit.

Message: No room in directory for file
Associated Command: EDLIN
Cause: This error message is displayed when you try to save a file in the root directory and it is full. Subdirectories are not limited in size as is the root directory.
Cure: Delete extraneous files from the root directory, or specify a filename in a subdirectory and reenter your text into EDLIN.

Message: Not enough room to merge the entire file
Associated Command: EDLIN
Cause: This error message is displayed if there is not enough room in memory to hold the file during a transfer command.
Cure: Free some memory by writing some files to disk. Then, reenter the transfer command.

Message: Not found
Associated Command: EDLIN
Cause: This error message is displayed if you enter a search or replace command that is unable to find a further occurrence of the specified search or replace string.
Cure: No action required.

Error Messages

Message: O.K.?
Associated Command: EDLIN
Cause: This prompt occurs during search and replace command processing.
Cure: Press any key except Y or N to continue the search or replace process.

Message: Too many files open
Associated Command: EDLIN
Cause: This error message is displayed when DOS cannot open the file to edit on the .BAK file due to lack of system file handles.
Cure: Increase the value of the FILES command in the CONFIG.SYS file.

EXE2BIN

Message: File cannot be converted
Associated Command: EXE2BIN
Cause: This error message is displayed when the input file is not in the correct format.

Message: Fixups needed - base segment <hex:>
Associated Command: EXE2BIN
Cause: This error message is displayed if the source (.EXE) file contains information indicating that a load segment is required for the file.
Cure: Specify the absolute segment address at which the finished module is to be located.

Message: Warning: Read error in EXE file
Associated Command: EXE2BIN
Cause: This error message is displayed when the amount read is less than the size of the header. This is a warning message only.
Cure: No action required.

APPENDIX E

FC

Message: Bad file
Associated Command: FC
Cause: The message is displayed when FC finds a defect in one of the files specified.
Cure: Run CHKDSK to verify the integrity of your disk.

Message: Data left in <fn.ft>
Associated Command: FC
Cause: This informational message is displayed if there is data left in one of the files being compared after the end of the other file is reached.
Cure: No action required.

Message: Files are different
Associated Command: FC
Cause: This error message is displayed after it detects a number of differences and gives up attempting to compare the files.
Cure: Edit the files to remove the reported differences and try again.

Message: Internal error
Associated Command: FC
Cause: This error message indicates an internal logic error in the FC utility.
Cure: Use COMP to compare your files.

FIND

Message: Find: File not found <fn.ft>
Associated Command: FIND
Cause: This error message is displayed when you specify a file that doesn't exist.
Cure: Make sure you type the filename correctly.

Error Messages

Message: Find: Invalid number of parameters
Associated Command: FIND
Cause: This error message is displayed if you specify too many or too few options on the command line.

Message: Find: Invalid Parameter
Associated Command: FIND
Cause: This error message is displayed if one of the options you specified is wrong.
Cure: Reenter the command correctly.

Message: Find: Read error in <fn.ft>
Associated Command: FIND
Cause: This error message is displayed if the program can't read the specified file.
Cure: Run CHKDSK to ensure the integrity of the disk and try again.

Message: Syntax error
Associated Command: FIND
Cause: You have typed a command line that FIND cannot interpret.
Cure: Check to make sure you typed the command line correctly.

FORMAT

Message: Cannot format an Assigned drive
Associated Command: FORMAT
Cause: This error message is displayed when a drive with an active assignment is specified as the target drive.
Cure: Use the ASSIGN command to clear the assignment and reenter the FORMAT command.

Message: Disk unsuitable for system drive
Associated Command: FORMAT
Cause: This error message is displayed if it detects a bad track on the disk where the system files should reside.

Cure: This disk should only be used for data. Use another disk if you want to make a system disk.

Message: Drive letter must be specified
Associated Command: FORMAT
Cause: You are trying to format a disk without specifying the drive that contains the disk. This prevents you from accidentally formatting the disk in the active drive.
Cure: Reenter the command with a drive specified.

Message: Enter current Volume Label for drive
  <x:>
Associated Command: FORMAT
Cause: FORMAT asks you to enter the current volume label for verification before it formats the hard disk in the specified drive.
Cure: Enter the current volume label for the hard disk. If you can't remember the current volume label, use the DIR command to display it and then reenter the FORMAT command.

Message: Format failure
Associated Command: FORMAT
Cause: This error message is displayed when DOS can't format a disk. The message is usually displayed with an explanation as to why DOS can't format the disk.
Cure: Restart the FORMAT command.

Message: Insert DOS diskette into drive <x:>
  and strike any key when ready
Associated Command: FORMAT
Cause: This error message is displayed when you specify the /S option and the disk in the default drive does not contain the DOS system files.
Cure: Insert the disk the contains the IBMBIO.COM and IBMDOS.COM files (or the equivalent files on an MS DOS disk) in the specified drive.

Message: Insert new diskette for drive <x:>
  and strike any key when ready
Associated Command: FORMAT

Error Messages

Cause: This error message is displayed when you need to insert a blank disk into the appropriate drive.

Cure: Press any character or number key to begin formatting. If there is any data on the disk, it is destroyed by the format process.

Message: Insufficient memory for system transfer Processing cannot continue

Associated Command: FORMAT

Cause: This error message is displayed when the memory configuration is insufficient to transfer the DOS system files IBMBIO.COM and IBMDOS.COM (or the equivalent MS DOS files) when using the /S option.

Cure: Reboot the system with fewer device drivers or more memory.

Message: Invalid characters in volume label

Associated Command: FORMAT

Cause: This error message is displayed when the volume label contains too many characters or invalid characters.

Cure: Use the LABEL command to ensure the volume label contains no more than 11 alphanumeric characters.

Message: Press any key to begin formatting <x:>

Associated Command: FORMAT

Cause: This prompt is issued before DOS begins formatting a disk.

Cure: Press any character or number to begin the format process. To end this command, press CTRL-C.

Message: Reinsert diskette for drive <x:>

Associated Command: FORMAT

Cause: This message is displayed when you need to reinsert the disk being formatted in the indicated drive.

Cure: Insert the disk to be formatted in the specified drive.

Message: Track 0 bad - disk unusable

Associated Command: FORMAT

Cause: The FORMAT command cannot accommodate defective sectors on the disk near the beginning.
Cure: Try formatting another disk.

Message: Volume label (11 characters, ENTER for none)?
Associated Command: FORMAT
Cause: This message is displayed when you specify the /V option in the FORMAT command.
Cure: Specify a volume label or press N to indicate that you do not want a volume label for the disk.

Message: WARNING, ALL DATA ON NONRE-MOVABLE DISK
DRIVE <x:> WILL BE LOST!
Proceed with Format (Y/N)?
Associated Command: FORMAT
Cause: This error message is displayed when there is data on the hard disk that you are trying to format.
Cure: If you want to erase the data and format the disk, press Y. If you do not want the files on your hard disk erased, press N, copy the files to a flexible disk, and then repeat the FORMAT command.

MODE

Message: Invalid baud rate specified
Associated Command: MODE
Cause: This error message is displayed if a baud rate other than 110, 150, 300, 600, 1200, 2400, 4800, 9600, or 19200 is specified.
Cure: Reenter the command with a valid baud rate.

Message: Port not installed
Associated Command: MODE
Cause: This error message is displayed if the port specified (LPTn: or COMn:) is not present on the system.
Cure: Specify a port that exists on the system and reenter command line.

Message: ABORTED - Assigned Port # missing or invalid
Associated Command: MODE
Cause: This error message is displayed when you are redirecting printer output with the MODE command and the serial port is not on the system or the port is not COM1:, COM2:, COM3:, or COM4:.
Cure: Reenter command line.

Message: ABORTED - Bad device parameter keyword
Associated Command: MODE
Cause: This error message is displayed when a device other than LPT: or COM: is specified on the command. MODE only affects the parallel ports, serial ports, and screen.
Cure: Reenter command line.

Message: ABORTED - Illegal BUSY value
Associated Command: MODE
Cause: This error message is displayed when something other than P is specified to initialize a port as the printer device.
Cure: Reenter command line.

Message: ABORTED - Illegal STOPBITS value
Associated Command: MODE
Cause: This error message is displayed when a value other than 1 or 2 is specified as the number of stop bits.
Cure: Reenter command line.

Message: ABORTED - Illegal DATABITS value
Associated Command: MODE
Cause: This error message is displayed when a value other than 7 or 8 is specified as the number of data bits.
Cure: Reenter command line.

Message: ABORTED - Invalid Switch
Associated Command: MODE

Cause: This error message is displayed when an invalid option is specified on the command line.
Cure: Reenter command line.

MORE

Message: —More—
Associated Command: MORE
Cause: The program that piped its output to MORE has produced more than one screen of data for MORE to print.
Cure: Press the space bar to view more of the file or directory.

Message: MORE: Incorrect DOS version
Associated Command: MORE
Cause: This error message is displayed because MORE won't run on versions of DOS prior to 3.2.
Cure: Use the correct versions of MORE and DOS.

Message: Must specify destination line number
Associated Command: MORE
Cause: This error message is displayed when you need to specify a destination line number when copying and inserting lines with EDLIN.
Cure: Reenter the command with the destination line.

PRINT

Message: All files canceled by operator
Associated Command: PRINT
Cause: This is an informational message displayed when the /T (terminate queue) option is specified.
Cure: No action required.

Message: Cannot open <fn.ft>
Associated Command: PRINT

Error Messages

Cause: This error message is displayed when the specified file cannot be found in an accessible directory.

Cure: Make sure that the filename is correctly entered on the command line, or move the file into an accessible directory.

Message: Errors on list device indicate that it may be offline. Please check it.

Associated Command: PRINT

Cause: This message is displayed if a printer time-out error is detected. This error can also be displayed during a long printer operation such as a form feed. This message is displayed only when the PRINT command is executed.

Cure: Turn the printer on or return it to an online status if appropriate. If the error occurs during a long printer operation, ignore the message.

Message: <fn.ft> canceled by operator

Associated Command: PRINT

Cause: This message is printed on the printer when you specify the /T switch in the PRINT command.

Message: <fn.ft> file not found

Associated Command: PRINT

Cause: This error message is displayed if disks are switched while a file is queued up, but before it starts to print.

Cure: Reenter the PRINT command for that file.

Message: <fn.ft> is currently being printed

Associated Command: PRINT

Cause: This error message is displayed when the file specified is being printed.

Cure: No action required.

Message: <fn.ft> is in queue

Associated Command: PRINT

Cause: This error message is displayed when the file specified is waiting to be printed.

Cure: No action required.

Message: Output is not assigned to a device
Associated Command: PRINT
Cause: This error message is displayed if PRINT is set up for a device that doesn't exist.
Cure: Specify a valid device name.

Message: Name of list device (PRN):
Associated Command: PRINT
Cause: This prompt appears the first time PRINT is run. Any valid device can be specified; that device then becomes the PRINT output device.
Cure: Specify the device you want to use to print.

Message: No files match d:<fn.ft>
Associated Command: PRINT
Cause: This error message is displayed when you want to add a file to the queue, but no filename matches the specification.
Cure: Reenter the command with a valid filename.

Message: PRINT queue is empty
Associated Command: PRINT
Cause: This error message is displayed when there aren't any files waiting to be printed.
Cure: No action required.

Message: PRINT queue is full
Associated Command: PRINT
Cause: This error message is displayed when there is no room in the list of files waiting to be printed.
Cure: Wait until some of the waiting files are printed, or remove them from the queue. Reenter the PRINT command.

Message: Resident part of PRINT installed
Associated Command: PRINT
Cause: This is the first message that DOS displays when you issue the PRINT command. It means that available memory has been reduced by several thousand bytes to process the PRINT command concurrent with other processes.
Cure: No action required.

Error Messages

RECOVER

Message: Press any key to begin recovery of the file(s) on drive <x:>
Associated Command: RECOVER
Cause: This prompt is issued before you recover a disk or file.
Cure: Press any character or number to begin the recover process. To end this command, press Enter.

Message: Warning - directory full
Associated Command: RECOVER
Cause: This error message is displayed when the root directory is too full for RECOVER processing.
Cure: Delete some files in the root directory to free space.

Message: <x> of <x> Bytes recovered
Associated Command: RECOVER
Cause: This error message tells you how many bytes DOS was able to recover of the disk or file.

RENAME

Message: Duplicate file name or File not found
Associated Command: RENAME
Cause: Either the new filename already exists or the file being renamed doesn't exist.
Cure: Make sure the new filename doesn't already exist or make sure the file being renamed does exist.

REPLACE

Message: Parameters not compatible
Associated Command: REPLACE
Cause: This message is displayed when you enter invalid or incorrect parameters.

Cure: Reenter the command using the correct syntax and valid parameters.

Message: No files found <fn.ft>
Associated Command: REPLACE
Cause: This message is displayed if it can't find matching source or target files.
Cure: Reenter the command with the correct source or target filenames.

Message: Source path required
Associated Command: REPLACE
Cause: This message is displayed when the correct source path isn't specified.
Cure: Reenter the command using the correct source path.

RMDIR

Message: Invalid path, not directory, or directory not empty
Associated Command: RMDIR
Cause: This error message is displayed when you are unable to remove the directory requested for one of the specified reasons.
Cure: Make sure the directory actually exists and is empty. Then, reenter the command.

SELECT

Message: Cannot find or execute <x:> FORMAT.COM
Associated Command: SELECT
Cause: This message is displayed when it is unable to execute the FORMAT command. Either the FORMAT command is missing or you do not have enough memory to load it.
Cure: Make sure the FORMAT command is on the disk in the source drive.

Message: Cannot find or execute d: XCOPY.EXE
Associated Command: SELECT
Cause: This message is displayed when it is unable to execute the XCOPY command. Either the XCOPY command is missing or you do not have enough memory to load it.
Cure: Make sure the XCOPY command is on the disk in the source drive.

Message: Error while copying files
Associated Command: SELECT
Cause: This message is displayed when it runs into an error while executing the XCOPY command. The target disk may be out of room or you may have specified an incorrect path.
Cure: If the target disk doesn't have enough space for the files, rerun the SELECT command on a larger capacity blank disk (in a compatible drive). Also, make sure that you don't specify a path that incorporates the same name as one of the system files you are copying over.

Message: Error while formatting target disk
Associated Command: SELECT
Cause: SELECT received an error while formatting the target disk. (The nature of the error should be listed in the error message.)
Cure: Correct the problem listed in the error message and reenter the command.

Message: Error while making CONFIG.SYS and AUTOEXEC.BAT
Associated Command: SELECT
Cause: There probably is not enough room on the target disk.
Cure: Try a larger capacity disk in a compatible drive. Then reenter the command.

Message: Incorrect number of parameters
Associated Command: SELECT

APPENDIX E

Cause: You entered too few or too many parameters.
(The valid number of parameters is from 2 to 4).
Cure: Reenter the command with the correct number of parameters.

Message: Invalid keyboard code
Associated Command: SELECT
Cause: You specified an invalid keyboard code.
Cure: Reenter the command with a valid keyboard code.
Refer to the SELECT command description in this manual for a list of valid keyboard codes.

Message: Invalid parameter. The last two parameters must be country code and keyboard code.
Associated Command: SELECT
Cause: You entered parameters out of order.
Cure: Reenter the command using the correct syntax and order.

Message: Invalid path or path too long.
Associated Command: SELECT
Cause: You specified a path which contains invalid characters or is longer than 64 characters.
Cure: Reenter the command using only valid characters (see section in this manual on Invalid Characters) and a shorter path.

Message: Invalid source drive, must be A or B
Associated Command: SELECT
Cause: You specified an invalid source drive. Drives A: and B: are the only valid source drives for this command.
Cure: Reenter the command with a valid source drive.

Message: Invalid target drive
Associated Command: SELECT
Cause: You specified an invalid or nonexistent target drive.
Cure: Reenter the command using a valid drive designator (A:, B:, C:, and so on).

Error Messages

Message: Is KEYB.COM available on another disk? (Y/N)

Associated Command: SELECT

Cause: You specified a non-U.S. keyboard and the driver for that keyboard isn't on the disk in the source drive.

Cure: If you have the driver on another disk, enter Y and wait until you are prompted to insert the disk. If you don't have the driver, enter N and the program will abort. Refer to the SELECT command description in this manual for a list of the available keyboard codes.

Message: Source drive must be different from target drive. If no source drive is specified, it defaults to A:

Associated Command: SELECT

Cause: You specified the same drive designator for both the source and target drives. The source and target drives must be different.

Cure: Reenter the command using the correct syntax (only drive A: or drive B: can be the source drive). Note that if you do not enter a source drive, SELECT automatically assumes the source drive is drive A:. Therefore, the command line SELECT A: 1 US would result in an error.

Message: The file is not in the root directory of this disk.

Associated Command: SELECT

Cause: This message is displayed when it can't find the keyboard driver in the root directory of the source disk.

Cure: Make sure the keyboard driver you want is in the root directory of the source disk by using the DIR command. If the driver you want is in a subdirectory, copy it to the root directory and reenter the command.

SORT

Message: Sort: Incorrect DOS version
Associated Command: SORT
Cause: This error message is displayed if you try to run SORT on any version of DOS less than 3.2.
Cure: Use the correct versions of SORT and DOS.

Message: SORT: Insufficient disk space
Associated Command: SORT
Cause: This error message is displayed when the disk is full.
Cure: Remove some extraneous files from the disk and try again.

Message: SORT: Insufficient memory
Associated Command: SORT
Cause: This error message is displayed when there is not enough memory to run the SORT command.
Cure: Reduce the amount of data to be sorted and try again.

SYS

Message: Has invalid cluster, file truncated
Associated Command: SYS
Cause: This error message is displayed when the system files IBMBIO.COM and IBMDOS.COM (or the equivalent MS DOS files) occupy more space on the source disk than is available on the target disk.
Cure: No action required.

Message: Insert system diskette in drive <x:> and strike any key when ready.
Associated Command: SYS
Cause: This error message is displayed when SYS needs a disk from which to read the IBMBIO.COM and IBMDOS.COM files (or the equivalent MS DOS files) into memory.

Cure: Press any character or number key to start the system copy process.

Message: No room for system on destination disk
Associated Command: SYS
Cause: This error message is displayed when there is not enough room for the system files on the target disk.
Cure: Delete some files to make room for the system files or use another disk. You may need to reformat the disk to put the system files on it.

VDISK

Message: Buffer size adjusted
Associated Command: VDISK
Cause: This informational message is displayed when it is necessary to adjust the buffer size specified in the DEVICE=VDISK.SYS command in the CONFIG.SYS file.
Cure: Change buffer size if necessary.

Message: Directory entries adjusted
Associated Command: VDISK
Cause: This informational message is displayed when it is necessary to adjust the number of directory entries specified in the DEVICE=VDISK.SYS command in the CONFIG.SYS file.
Cure: Change the number of directory entries if necessary.

Message: Invalid switch character
Associated Command: VDISK
Cause: This error message is displayed if the switch specified isn't /E. VDISK attempts to install the virtual disk in low memory.
Cure: Reenter the command in the CONFIG.SYS file.

Message: Sector size adjusted
Associated Command: VDISK

Cause: This informational message is displayed when it is necessary to adjust the sector size specified in the DEVICE=VDISK.SYS command in the CONFIG.SYS file.
Cure: Change sector size, if necessary.

Message: VDISK not installed - buffer too small
Associated Command: VDISK
Cause: This error message is displayed when the virtual disk drive cannot be installed due to an incorrect buffer size.
Cure: Change the buffer size, if necessary.

Message: VDISK not installed - insufficient memory
Associated Command: VDISK
Cause: This error message is displayed when the virtual disk drive cannot be installed due to insufficient memory. If less than 64K of system memory would be left after the virtual disk is installed, this message is displayed.
Cure: Change the buffer size, if necessary.

Message: VDISK not installed - no extended memory
Associated Command: VDISK
Cause: This error message is displayed when the /E option is specified, but the system does not have extended memory, or the amount of available extended memory is insufficient to contain the virtual disk even after adjusting the parameters.
Cure: Ensure that you have enough extended memory to run VDISK, or reduce the size of the VDISK.

XCOPY

Message: Cannot COPY to (or from) a reserved device
Associated Command: XCOPY
Cause: You can't use XCOPY to copy to or from a device (for instance CON or PRN).

Cure: Reenter the command copying to or from a file instead of a device.

Message: Cannot perform a cyclic copy
Associated Command: XCOPY
Cause: This message is displayed when you specify the /S switch and a target that is a subdirectory of the source.
Cure: Do not specify a target that is a subdirectory of the source when using the /S switch.

Message: <fn.ft> File not found
Associated Command: XCOPY
Cause: This message is displayed when DOS cannot find the file that you specified.
Cure: Make sure that the path is correct and the file exists in the directory you specified.

Message: Invalid path
Associated Command: XCOPY
Cause: You specified a source path that lists a subdirectory that doesn't exist.
Cure: Specify a source path that lists a subdirectory that does exist.

Message: Too many open files
Associated Command: XCOPY
Cause: This error message is displayed when DOS cannot open the XCOPY command file due to a lack of system file handles.
Cure: Increase the value of the FILES command in the CONFIG.SYS file.

Message: Unable to create directory
Associated Command: XCOPY
Cause: This message is displayed when DOS can't create the directory you specified.
Cure: Check for a filename conflict (you may have a file with the same name you want to use for your directory). Or, the disk may be full, in which case you can either delete files no longer needed or use a higher capacity disk in a compatible drive.

APPENDIX E

Miscellaneous Error Messages

The following error messages are associated with more than one command.

Message: Access denied
Associated Commands: REPLACE, XCOPY
Cause: You tried to overwrite a read-only file.
Cure: Change the status of the read-only file using the ATTRIB command and then reenter the command.

Message: Are you sure (Y/N)?
Associated Commands: DEL, ERASE, FORMAT
Cause: This cautionary message is displayed if you instruct DOS to delete all of the files in a directory. This message is also displayed by FORMAT if you instruct it to format Drive C: (the hard disk).
Cure: Enter Y if you want to proceed or N if you don't.

Message: Drive <x:> not ready.
Associated Commands: DISKCOMP, DISKCOPY
Cause: One of the disk drives is not ready.
Cure: If there is a disk in the drive, open the door, reinsert the disk, and reclose the door.

Message: File allocation table bad drive <x:>
Associated Commands: CHKDSK, PRINT
Cause: This error message is displayed when a disk may be defective.
Cure: Run CHKDSK to check the disk.

Message: File not found
Associated Commands: EDLIN, EXE2BIN, FC, FIND, DOS, RECOVER, REN
Cause: This error message is displayed when DOS cannot find the file that you specified.
Cure: Make sure that the path is accurate and the file exists in the directory you specified.

Message: Incorrect number of parameters
Associated Commands: JOIN, SUBST

Cause: This error message is displayed when you specify too many or too few options on the command line.
Cure: Reenter the command correctly.

Message: Incorrect parameter
Associated Commands: ASSIGN, SELECT, SHARE
Cause: This error message is displayed when one of the options you specified, or the syntax you used, was wrong.
Cure: Reenter the command correctly.

Message: Insert diskette with COMMAND.COM in drive <x:> and strike a key when ready
Associated Commands: DISKCOMP, DISKCOPY
Cause: DOS is trying to load the command processor COMMAND.COM, but it isn't in the drive from which you started your system.
Cure: Insert the DOS disk in the indicated drive and press any key.

Message: Insufficient disk space
Associated Commands: EXE2BIN, DOS, REPLACE, SORT, XCOPY
Cause: This error message is displayed when the disk is full. It does not contain enough room to perform the specified operation.
Cure: Delete nonessential files from the disk and try again, or, in the case of XCOPY, use a higher capacity disk in a compatible drive.

Message: Insufficient memory
Associated Commands: REPLACE, XCOPY
Cause: This message is displayed when there is not enough memory to run the program.
Cure: REPLACE or XCOPY fewer files at a time, or one at a time.

Message: Invalid country code
Associated Commands: COUNTRY, SELECT
Cause: This error message is displayed when you specify a country code that is not on the list of valid country

codes for this version of DOS.
Cure: See the COUNTRY or SELECT command for a list of valid country codes.

Message: Invalid drive or filename
Associated Commands: EDLIN, RECOVER
Cause: This error message is displayed when a valid drive or a valid filename needs to be specified.
Cure: Specify a valid drive or filename.

Message: Invalid drive specification
Associated Commands: CHKDSK, FORMAT, REPLACE, SYS, XCOPY
Cause: This error message is displayed when a valid drive needs to be specified.
Cure: Specify a valid drive.

Message: Invalid number of parameters
Associated Commands: FC, FIND, RECOVER, XCOPY
Cause: This error message is displayed when the wrong number of options are specified on the command line.
Cure: Reenter the command with the correct number of options.

Message: Invalid parameter
Associated Commands: CHKDSK, EDLIN, FC, FIND, FORMAT, PRINT, REPLACE, SELECT, XCOPY
Cause: This error message is displayed when one of the options specified is wrong.
Cure: Check the correct syntax and reenter the command.

Message: Not enough memory
Associated Commands: JOIN, SHARE, SUBST
Cause: This error message is displayed when there is not enough memory for DOS to run the command.
Cure: Reduce the number of installed drives and virtual disks, or acquire more memory for your system.

Message: Path not found
Associated Commands: CHKDSK, REPLACE, XCOPY

Cause: This error message is displayed when you specify an invalid path.
Cure: Make sure you enter the path correctly and the path exists.

Message: Path too long
Associated Commands: REPLACE, XCOPY
Cause: The specified path is too long.
Cure: Change subdirectories to REPLACE or XCOPY files in lower level subdirectories.

Message: Read error in <fn.ft>
Associated Commands: FC, FIND
Cause: This error message is displayed when DOS cannot read the file.
Cure: Run CHKDSK to ensure the integrity of the files. RECOVER them, if necessary.

Message: System transferred
Associated Commands: FORMAT, SYS
Cause: This error message is displayed when the system files IBMDOS.COM and IBMBIO.COM are transferred during FORMAT and SYS command processing.
Cure: No action required.

Message: Unrecoverable Read Error on Drive <x:> Side y, Track z
Associated Commands: DISKCOMP, DISKCOPY
Cause: This error message is displayed after several unsuccessful attempts are made to read the data from the specified track and sector on the disk in the indicated drive.
Cure: The disk is bad. RECOVER as many files as possible, copy the files to another disk, and try reformatting.

Index